Practical Guide to Everyday Carry Gear

Interviews by **ROB ROBIDEAU**

Published by the Personal Armament Network

Contents

Selecting A Handgun for EDC

Massad Ayoob has been the handgun editor of GUNS magazine and law enforcement editor of AMERICAN HANDGUNNER since the 1970s, and has published thousands of articles in gun magazines, martial arts publications, and law enforcement journals. He is the author of more than a dozen books on firearms, self-defense, and related topics, including "In the Gravest Extreme," widely considered to be the authoritative text on the topic of the use of lethal force.

The winner of the Outstanding American Handgunner of the Year Award in 1998, Mas has won several state and regional handgun shooting championships. Ayoob is one of approximately ten Five Gun Masters among the 10,000-member International Defensive Pistol Association, and was the first to earn that title. He served 19 years as chair of the Firearms Committee of the American Society of Law Enforcement Trainers, and several years as a member of the Advisory Board of the International Law Enforcement Educators and Trainers Association. In addition to teaching for those groups, he has also taught for the International Association of Law Enforcement Firearms Instructors and the International Homicide Investigators seminars.

Mas has received judicial recognition as an expert witness for the courts in weapons and shooting cases since 1979, and has been a fully sworn and empowered, part time police officer for 36 years. Ayoob founded the Lethal Force Institute in 1981 and served as its director until 2009, and now trains through Massad Ayoob Group.

He has appeared on CLE-TV delivering continuing legal education for attorneys, through the American Law Institute and American Bar Association, and has been retained to train attorneys to handle deadly force cases through the Armed Citizens Legal Defense Network. Ayoob served for two years as co-vice chair of the Forensic Evidence Committee of the National Association of Criminal Defense Lawyers. He also appears in each episode of Personal Defense TV (Sportsman's Channel).

Rob: After reading a lot of your work, I'd say that your specialty is examining, commentating on, and breaking down armed conflict, but today we're going to take a slightly different direction with you. I think this might be even a little bit more fun. I want to talk to you about the gear associated with concealed carry.

Mas: Okay.

Rob: There are several people that are at the point where they're choosing gear for concealed carry. Some of these people have been shooting for years, maybe even since childhood. Maybe they've been hunting, or into handguns also, but finally they realize the need to conceal carry a handgun. Now they're looking at something that's totally different than just a range gun. On the other hand, there are some people that have never shot before, and they've come to the same conclusion: They need to conceal carry a handgun. They're looking for gear also. So we're going to try to address both of these people. They have different backgrounds, they're going to have different thought processes, but what is the first step in that decision? Where do people start when they're looking at their concealed carry gear, trying to select it?

Mas: Well, the first step, of course, is to decide that you are going to be armed. To come to terms with the fact that you may one day have to use the lethal weapon in a lethal way. To make certain that you have enough knowledge and training in the field that you know when it's time and when it's not time to be taking it out, when it's time and not time to be pulling the trigger. Once that's accomplished and we are just looking at hardware, you want to be looking, at what fits you. None of us would buy an automobile that didn't have adjustable seats if the steering wheel and seat were set for somebody six inches or a foot taller then we were. I see an amazing number of people who are! Their buddy had a Beretta 92 (which is an outstanding pistol and one of my own favorites), so they figure that must be the best and they get one, but their finger is one digit shorter than their buddy's and the Beretta(which has a long trigger reach) doesn't suit them. There might be other guns in the Beretta catalogue, and many other catalogues, that would fit them better.

We also need to look at the holster selection. Ideally, you would carry the gun in one place all the time. Unfortunately, life is not ideal. We all have our own favorite, most comfortable clothes for any given season, but there are also times that we have to put on the necktie, the tight collared dress shirt, and the monkey suit to go to church, to go to the wedding, to go to court, or whatever. You will find as you go about being armed 24/7 that the carry code follows the dress code. There are guns that I can conceal in a pair of elastic waist BDUs with a good belt, and a one size larger then I'd normally wear T-shirt untucked. Heck, I can carry a full-sized 1911 government model .45 or a full-sized Glock 17 or 22 in one of those, but if I'm in a situation where I have to dress for court and wear a tailored suit, I'm going to carry a smaller handgun in as discrete a holster as I can arrange.

There are two objectives when carrying the concealed weapon. "Weapon" is one operative term, but "concealed" is the other. The saying on the internet, "Concealed means concealed," is absolutely true. I see the occasional person who's carrying a full-sized, almost target-sized pistol in a $20 nylon holster that was designed essentially to be a gun case worn on the belt when you're at the range or out in the field. The thing basically looks like a giant gun with a small human being attached and a garment draped over it.

There's going to be some degree of investment in quality holsters and quality belts. Bear in mind that the gun and the system that carries it are synergistic. Having taught private citizens since 1981, and cops since 1972, I can't tell you how many people I've seen with the $1,000 gun and a $15 nylon holster whose brand should be Fruit-Of-The-Loom. The thing hangs out away from their body. It's a sloppy fit to the belt. When they try to draw the gun, the holster comes up with it, and somewhere around ribcage level the gun begins to separate from the holster.

The other thing I see is the guy with the $1,000 gun, the $100 top quality holster, and he's got the thing on a belt that looks like it's proof that you can skin a chicken, tan the hide, and made a belt out of it. The belt's institutional memory is probably the words, "Attention K-Mart shoppers." The fine gun and the fine holster will hang off the soft, narrow, floppy belt, and look, once again, like a gun with a small human being attached. When they go for their gun, the holster will come up with the gun, and at some point around the ribcage the belt will finally allow the holster to yield the gun.

I'd much rather see somebody with a less expensive, good-quality handgun and a decent quality holster. You can get decent quality holsters today in the $30 range. Put it on a good, solid belt that'll hold the whole thing. The guys who get the $2,000 pistol and the cheap crappy holster and belt, is like saving up to buy a Mercedes Benz so your family would have the safest automobile, then you put on two ply retread tires to save a few bucks. You missed the whole point.

Rob: Let's go back to what you were saying about fitting the handgun. You've covered a lot of ground here. I just want to kind of emphasize these different points. You're saying that there is no unequivocally best handgun for everybody. It doesn't matter what your best buddy says about his gun and how cool it is and how great it is for him. It doesn't do any good if it doesn't fit you and it doesn't work for you.

Mas: There are elements of size, and there are also elements of need. Your buddy might be like I am. I've been a handgun retention instructor for 30-some years now. I am not at all uncomfortable carrying a gun in an open top holster. Literally a few hundred to over a 1,000 times a year, I will demonstrate gun retention techniques, which means 1,000 repetitions hand to hand of someone trying to take the gun away from me. Obviously it's going to be an unworkable dummy gun, but the practice and the habituation are there. Most people don't have that.

A number of people, particularly those worrying about being disarmed, might be better served with a pistol that has a manual safety. With a reasonable amount of practice time taking the safety off and on, anything from the 1911 to a Beretta becomes second nature for the user, but there is one thing we've discovered over the years about when the bad guy gets the gun away from the good guy. Unless the bad guy is very familiar with that particular type of pistol, which is not usually the case, they spend a considerable amount of time fumbling with it, trying to figure out where the switch is that turns this thing on, because I'm pulling on the trigger and it's not working.

In the studies over the years, the first one was done in the early 1980s and published in *Police Chief Magazine*, they essentially took a study group of everything from people who had some familiarity with guns to people who had never touched one. They put them on a shooting range and put two loaded guns in front of them: a Smith & Wesson double action revolver and a cocked and locked Colt .45 auto. There was a silhouette target just three or four feet away and with the camera and timers going, they said, "Okay, when the buzzer goes off, pick up that gun, shoot the target, and let's see how long it takes."

The average person was able to grab the gun, point it, and pull the trigger with the double action revolver in approximately 1.2 seconds. It took an average of 16.9 seconds when they grabbed the on-safe Colt. An average of 16.9 seconds to figure out which of these buttons, levers, and whistles makes the gun go bang! Now for the legitimate shooter, from the days of Jeff Cooper in the 1950s to Rob Leatham today, the speed records have been set with cocked and locked 1911 pistols in the hands of people who understood that as the gun is coming up and I intend to fire, my thumb will close down, swipe the safety into the fire position, and I'll break the shot. It's pretty clear that for the competent committed person, there's no significant loss of time in carrying a gun that's on safe.

This might be a concern for a great many people who fear they're at risk of being disarmed if they carry their own loaded gun, particularly the person who's new to it. Yet if you look in other parts of the world of the gun, I've met a lot of trap and skeet shooters who don't hunt, and the only time they ever shoot their shotguns is on the trap and skeet field.

Their shotgun has never been on safe. They've never felt a need to. They are not in the habit of taking the safety off on their firearm.

What I'm saying is, the person who carries concealed out and about in public is there because they have some expectation, however remote, that they might be in a lethal force confrontation. Those confrontations tend to be so close that the possibility of the other guy going for your gun is very real, and there are considerations that you take there that you might not take in some sport shooting situation, like bulls-eye pistol or trap and skeet.

Rob: I've heard some people talk about ergonomics like it's useless and worthless. That in the heat of the moment, in an armed encounter, your fine motor skills go to pot and you're stuck with just trying to grab it as best as you can. But personally, I believe that a good ergonomic set-up, something that fits you, is going to make that easier. How does someone go about making sure that their gun fits them? What aspects are they looking at? How are they checking this?

Mas: First, I totally agree with you. The fit of the gun to the hand is essentially the interface between the person and the machine. The better it fits, the more natural, the more reflexive they'll be with it. In a situation where their dexterity is falling through the floor, the gun will be more forgiving to the hand that grabs it sloppily.

I think the key dimension that we're looking at when we talk about the fit of a handgun to the hand is trigger reach. Trigger reach is measured on the hand from the center of the web of the hand, in line with the long bones of the forearm, to the contact point on the index finger where it's going to make contact with the trigger. This will vary. Instructor A may recommend the tip of the finger for contact, Instructor B, the pad of the finger, which I would define as the center of the whorl of the fingerprint, and Instructor C might advise the distal joint, the crease on the palmer surface of the index finger just before you reach the fingertip.

For me personally, on a defense gun which tends to have a heavier trigger, I much prefer distal joint placement. It's almost mandatory to do good work with a very heavy trigger gun like a double action revolver. This is especially true if you have a long trigger stroke like on a double action revolver a double-action-only semiautomatic pistol. On a semi-automatic pistol, the measurement is taken from just below the grip tang at the center of the back strap of the grip frame to the center of the trigger at the point where the finger would be making contact.

Rob: We're talking about the length of pull. This is something that you're not going to be able to just look at measurements and say, "Okay, that looks like that'll work! My size is X. I'm going to be able to fit this because I know they measured this gun." It's something you really have to go out there and shoot and try for yourself. See how it feels.

Mas: You really do. Look at the industry's response to the law enforcement sector. You and I can go into a gun shop, pick out 10 or 20 different guns, and find the one that our hand just says, "Ah, this is the one". Suppose you're the armorer or the firearm instructor for a police department with somewhere between 10 and 10,000 police officers. You've determined, or the bureaucracy has determined, that they must all be issued the same gun. Now we've got some problems, because you're going to have little people and large people. I've seen police officers who stand less than five feet tall and in the class that I just finished last night we had one police officer that was 6'6" with proportional sized hands.

One of the reasons we're seeing today the very strong rise in popularity in the Smith & Wesson Military and Police pistol in law enforcement is the interchangeable back straps that allow the dimension of trigger reach to be altered from the small hands it to large hands. Glock, our largest police pistol manufacturer, has picked up on this, and a couple of years ago introduced the Gen4 which has the same feature. I know a great many people who love the Glock pistol and are trading their older generation Glocks for the Gen4mply because it fits them better.

The Gen4 Glock, in the otherwise identical barrel length and caliber will allow more trigger reach. As the gun comes out of the box, just the bare frame, it is a shorter trigger reach, more suitable for the smaller hand. There are two inserts that go onto the back strap, one of which will bring it to the same trigger reach, essentially, that you had with Generation Two or Generation Three Glock pistols, and one more that, if you have an absolutely huge hand, will be kind of like taking a Glock 21 .45 and putting a rubber grip sleeve over it. You've got something that's going to fit virtually every hand. It is something important. It's something the industry has recognized, and it's something that the institutional handgun users, basically law enforcement, have recognized as well.

Rob: Here's something that you and I probably think is obvious, but I've had some people that have told me, "My hand is big enough. I can handle any gun," but just because your hand is large enough to completely wrap around it, it doesn't mean that you're not going to have a better grip with a gun that does have a larger diameter to wrap your hand around. Try grabbing a very tiny pen, and you're going to see how awkward it is. Just because your hand is big enough to fit around it and you can hold it, doesn't mean it's good for you. Large or small hands, you want to find something that's going to fit you.

Mas: Very true. As a general rule, the person with the larger hands, or when you're talking rifle and shotgun, the taller person with longer arms, can adapt to the smaller gun better than the smaller person can adapt to the larger. That said, it doesn't mean the very tiny guns are perfect for the large bodies or the large hands. Look at the little J-frame Smith & Wesson, which was essentially built on a 19th century .32 frame and built in .38 Special and now today .357 Magnum. A large-handed guy who grabs it with a barrel inline with the forearm will find the median joint of his trigger finger centered on the trigger, and when he pulls the trigger back, it will now tend to pull the gun very strongly to the side. Generations of large-handed male cops and private citizens who carried those guns for their compactness, have put on custom grips that had a spacer or a cushion behind the back strap that would push their hand back and give them more optimum trigger reach.

Rob: So let's talk about the system itself. When you look at a racecar, and trying to make a racecar perform at its best, they're going to look for the area that's weakest and try to strengthen it. There's the old saying that a chain is only as strong as its weakest link, and that's kind of the way that we should look at our concealed carry system. You mentioned the belt, the holster, these different aspects. None of them is more important than the other. It's important that you make sure that they're all working together, and one of them is not far behind the others.

Mas: Exactly. The other thing, continuing your analogy of the race driver, are we doing Indy 500, the Bonneville Salt Flats, or a long distance rally race on winding mountain roads? That's going to change everything from the choice of vehicle to the choice of tires to the techniques and tactics of driving the machine.

Rob: I know this may sound odd for someone that doesn't understand this, but many people end up spending just as much on the gear that goes with their gun as they do on the gun itself: Extra magazines, holsters, a good belt..

Mas: Absolutely. Among our friends the riflemen, the saying is, "You tell the real professional rifleman by the fact that he probably paid more for his telescopic sight than he did for the rifle itself."

Rob: So when you're looking at these things, where do you go first? Where do people start with selecting a good holster?

Mas: You want to have it where you can reach it, and we've got to look at both wardrobe and body shape. For example, in the old days, back in the 1950s, there were a number of police departments around the country, both highway patrols, county departments like Metro Dade, and some city police departments that issued cross-draw holsters with the gun carried on the opposite side of the dominant hand with the butt forward. The rationale was that for the right-handed officer or trooper, if you're transporting a suspect in the front seat your gun was farther away from them, but you could still reach it by reaching across your body. If you had to shoot out the window, you could drive with your right hand, turn your left hand palm outward, draw from the left hip with the butt forward in what's called cavalry draw, and shoot out the window. Unfortunately, they discovered that a great many males simply did not have the range of movement, particularly the big, broad-shouldered guys, to reach the gun from there.

They found also when you were facing someone, the butt was presented to them, and they could literally reach your gun faster than you in an attempt to disarm you. So today, virtually every American police officer will carry on the dominant side, the strong side, hip.

We have found over the years that the tendency has historically been that American private citizens will model their choice of rifle on what the military uses. We see that so classically today with the AR-15 platform. And that historically, again, the private citizen would model on domestic law enforcement for their choice of defensive firearm. Perhaps partly because police tend to carry strong side hip, the great majority of private citizens, at least the ones I train, carry strong side hip. I make it clear on the website and the literature the students get before they arrive, bring the gun that you carry.

There are a couple of things that I don't think are safe. I would not allow someone to draw from a middle of the back holster that held the barrel horizontal, because there's no safe way that gun can be drawn without the muzzle at some point crossing the person on your left(possibly also the person on your right) on the firing line. I do allow them to use cross-draw and shoulder holsters, and simply show them how to do it safely without crossing anyone with the muzzle. That said, it is extremely rare for me to see someone come to the range, or come to the class, with that type of holster. Usually, when I do, it'll be someone who's got a physical handicap that requires it. A torn rotator cuff on the gun-hand side shoulder will very much limit the ability for the elbow to come back and draw from behind the hip but does not impede a cross-draw from the front.

Now, you start looking at different body shapes. If you give the individual shooters a choice of what's more comfortable for them, you'll find a great many more females than males will be comfortable with the cross-draw holster and particularly with the shoulder holster. The reason for the cross-draw is that the hip holster was historically designed by males for males. The male will have proportionately, a much longer torso and lower hips. The male hips will tend to be fairly slim vis-à-vis the upper body. The female body, by its nature, has the flaring, higher hips and a shorter torso.

So the holster that was designed for you or I to draw from naturally and quickly, and will be very fast, natural, and concealable for us, will not be for a great many females. Where the butt on your or I is at kidney level, on them, the butt of the gun will be up by the floating ribs. While the barrel of that holstered gun on you or I would be pointed straight down, on them the flare of the hips pushes the muzzle outward and drives the upper part of the pistol, the back of the slide and the frame, into their lower ribcage area on their side. It's uncomfortable just sitting still, let alone carrying out strenuous activity, and they almost have to be a contortionist to draw the gun from there.

The cross-draw holster for you or I might be an awkward reach, because the hips are higher and because the torso is shorter. The female torso tends to be relatively narrower and they tend to have proportionately longer, more limber arms then you and I do, so they will find it absolutely comfortable reaching to the opposite hip.

Anything you and I would wear to anything from a wedding to the office to court will be pants with belt loops that we can put a suitable gun belt through and hold a pistol there. The female dress codes for the broad purposes of life and of work are not necessarily compatible with waist belts, but the shoulder holster, because it suspends off the shoulders, will fit in any female wardrobe that has some sort of an outer garment: everything from a light sweater to a women's business suit. I've found a great many women are much more comfortable with a shoulder rig then their brothers might be, even if the woman and the brother are the same height.

Rob: You mentioned that a lot of civilians want to be like the police officers, they want to be like the soldiers, but there is a slightly valid reason. When it comes to a military firearm, there is a decision making process. I hope that the government wasn't completely just bribed into selecting that firearm. There was some sort of a selection process that it went through. The same sort of process went with selecting the method of carry for officers. Is there validity in starting with that as your default? Start with strong-side hip, see how that goes? There's a reason that police officers and armed citizens have been doing this forever.

Mas: Yeah, and I think there is. It's not that they're saying wow, I want to be a cop or I want to be a soldier. I think it's exactly what you're saying, Rob, that they've looked at it and said here are a few million people in the military who found that gun to work for them. When we look at the concept of modeling off the police, that is even more valid. Obviously, there's little the American citizen does that follows the model of the American soldier. What the American citizen bought the gun for and carries the gun on the streets for comes much closer to what the law enforcement officer does. They are worried about the exact same criminals that the officers are out there facing.

They know that of all those cops, many of them will at some point be working in plain clothes and carrying the guns concealed just as they, the citizens, will, and that virtually all of them, at least at some point, will be carrying guns off duty in the same kind of clothing that they wear. It occurs to them that if 800,000 people have looked at this professionally and done studies on it, and they're carrying the gun where they are, why should I reinvent the wheel? It makes sense for me to carry it behind my hip, too.

This has pretty much become the default for the armed American citizen. You also see a great many folks carrying in pockets. I would say the second most common carry method would probably be pocket carry. If you're carrying in the pocket, do what any cop or trained professional would do and have it in a pocket holster. Have something that will protect the trigger guard from anything interdicting it and causing the gun to unintentionally discharge. The pocket holster will also break up the outline of the gun. Someone who looks very closely can see there's something in the pocket, but it might be a wallet, it might be a billfold, it might be a money clip, and nobody flags it as a gun. The pocket holster will do much to protect the gun from lint that could get in it and accumulate and cause a malfunction when you most desperately needed it to work. Another one of the big things with a pocket holster is that it keeps the gun from shifting position. You don't want to be reaching into your jeans pocket when your life is on the line and find your handgun has rotated upside down, and the muzzle is up and the butt is down. With a pocket holster it's always going to be in the same place, and the draw will be fast and clean.

Rob: After the holster, the next step, is the belt itself. This is something that a lot of people overlook. They think, "A belt is a belt." It holds your pants up, it holds your holster there, but there's a big difference between a leather dress belt and a belt that's meant to hold your gun where it needs to be.

Mas: Holding a light pair of pants up is a totally different task from holding what may be a couple of pounds or more of metal on one side of the belt that wants to tilt outward and away. You want to have a good, rigid belt, and there are several approaches to that. Some of the makers will put a plastic stiffener inside the belt. Some will do what's called the lined belt, essentially two layers of leather. Today we're seeing a lot of these synthetic belts, such as the Wilderness Belt that I wear a good deal of the time. It's rigid, it's comfortable, and it's much more adjustable than the conventional leather belt which has the tongue and hole belt buckle, because the Velcro attachment allows you to infinitely adjust. You don't have the half-inch of adjustment between the holes one way or the other. You can get it exactly perfect for where your body is that day with that particular holster.

Rob: And if you're carrying inside-the-waistband with different pants or different clothes, you may want it tighter or looser on different days. When you've got belt holes a half-inch away, you're not going to be able to set it up exactly how you want it.

Mas: For the inside the waistband holster, generations of people have tried them and said, "Wow, this is uncomfortable, this is too tight." No crap, Sherlock! You bought the pants to fit you, and now you are trying to fit you, the gun, and the holster. What I've found over decades of carrying inside the waistband, is that my pants are almost all two inches large in the waist. My normal waist size is a 32. Most of my pants are a 34. That allows me to very comfortably get the holstered gun inside the waistband. Inside-the-waistband carry is much more discrete, because now the outer garment can come all the way up to the belt and not reveal that you're carrying. The pants themselves are holding the holster against the body so you don't get the print of the shape of the gun that you might have with even the tightest to the body carry of an outside the waistband holster. It's more discrete for those who have discretion higher on their list than others.

There are certain police departments where the cops are casual about carrying. They've got their badge in front of the holster. They don't really much care if the gun becomes exposed. They're not going to frighten anybody, because anybody who sees the holstered gun is going to see the badge, know it's a cop, and not think they're being stalked by a criminal.

For the private citizen, we have a different paradigm entirely. A great many of my civilian, private citizen students, are people in the medical profession, legal profession, and executives, who are legally allowed to carry per se, but their particular professional culture or corporate culture is such that if they were discovered to be armed, the light weight yuppies who surround them, and in some cases are their supervisors, would be absolutely horrified. For the private citizen, discrete carry becomes a much higher priority on the checklist of values for a gun and holster selection than it might be for the off-duty police officer.

Rob: And that belt that keeps your system, your holster and your firearm, from being able to torque outward, goes a long way toward making sure that your system is actually concealable.

Mas: Absolutely true.

Rob: In many ways I'd say it's just as important as the selection of the actual firearm itself, because you could have a small firearm that the belt allows to hang out and protrude, and you're not going to be able to conceal that.

Mas: There is one thing every professional discovers, and it's been so since before I was born. If you have a small gun in a poorly chosen holster on a poorly chosen belt, it's going to bulge more then a full-sized service pistol in the best possible concealment holster that is secured on or inside the best possible belt. The longer barreled gun, in some cases, particularly inside the waistband, conceals better. That's because the short barreled gun, as it sits in the holster with its muzzle down and its butt up, has most of the weight above the belt. That tends to cause the gun to tilt outward a bit. With the longer barreled gun, the barrel of the gun itself bears on the hip and forces the butt of the gun in more toward the body. That's why you see so many of us who carry 24/7 and have been doing this for a living for a long time simply carrying full sized guns most of the time when they're concealed.

Rob: Let's talk about carrying extra magazines. There are a number of advantages of carrying extra magazines opposite your primary firearm. We're talking about belts and concealment. For me, carrying extra magazines opposite your firearm make it a lot easier for your belt not to ride up on one side, or just to stay even.

Mas: It literally balances you. Also, you always have to draw the line somewhere, but the person who has determined that it would be a good idea to have a gun, realizes that a gun without spare ammunition is a very temporary gun. There are any number of situations that could result in you needing more than 5 shots, more than 10 shots, or even, God help us all, more than 16 or 18 shots.

Particularly with a semiautomatic pistol, extra magazines are helpful if the gun malfunctions. Any professional instructor can tell you that a majority of handgun malfunctions tend to be related to the ammunition or the magazine, and any number of malfunctions can compromise the magazine. With a double-feed, for example, the topmost round in the magazine will be part way forward, trapped by the feed lips. If you press the mag release button, the magazine is not going to drop out like it would have normally. It is being held forward by the slide.

When you forcibly rip the magazine out, that can flip the topmost cartridge up. You occasionally see the rim get caught underneath the feed lips with the cartridge pointed straight up at 12:00, which of course means if you attempt to reinsert it, the gun will now hopelessly jam. The topmost cartridge, at best, will be forward in the feed lips, and if you try to reinsert it the way it is, it's going to jam the gun again once you've cleared the initial malfunction.

The simplest way to clear that type of malfunction is what we call, "Lock, rip, clear, reload, and go." You lock the slide back manually, you rip the spent magazine out of the gun, you work the slide until whatever's caught in the chamber has cleared through the ejection port, and then you simply grab another fresh magazine, slap it into the gun, rack the slide, and go back to work.

Rob: In a situation where you're deploying your handgun, you don't want to be picking at your magazine to make sure you can get it back into action.

Mas: It's the whole Murphy's Law thing. We don't carry the gun because there's an extreme likelihood we're going to need it on any given day. The odds tell us we probably won't. We carry it because of the absolutely catastrophic cost of that rare day when we needed it and didn't have it.

Rob: Because the likelihood of us using our firearm is in many cases so low, it's sometimes difficult for a lot of people to put themselves mentally into the situation where they would be using it so that they can take a practical look at what they need, what they're doing, how they're going to do things.

Mas: Essentially, it breeds complacency, and any cop can tell you complacency is what kills you. A young, rookie cop gets out of the academy all fired up. For the first month, every car he pulls over for going five miles over the speed limit or having a tail-light out, he's going to approach it like the entire Dillinger gang has come back from the dead and might be in the car. When you do that 100 times and another 100 times and another 100 times, and nobody attacks you, you start thinking, "Boy, this is foolish, this is paranoid," and you start dropping your guard. Pretty soon, you get out of the car and walk up to the stopped vehicle like you were walking in your own living room, and somewhere around the 1,000th time you do it, there's somebody in there who is desperately willing to kill you to stay free. You are now behind the curve. Complacency kills cops. Complacency kills anybody else who is in a dangerous situation that they've convinced themselves was never really going to happen.

Rob: We're talking about the gear aspect, but the mental aspects of considering the situation and game-planning it are just as important. There is a lot of good information out there on that subject also. I appreciate so much you taking the time here to talk about this.

Mas: I appreciate you caring enough about your listeners to bring up the topic. My book, *Gun Digest Guide Of Concealed Carry* is out and readily available. The entire book is devoted to tonight's topic, and that might be of interest. That's available from Digest Books, FW Publications, and can generally be found on Amazon or at Barnes & Noble.

Rob: You also write for several publications, right?

Mas: Yeah. I write each month for *American Handgunner, Guns Magazine, Combat Handguns, Guns and Weapons for Law Enforcement, Backwoods Home Magazine,* I'm their gun editor, *Shooting Industry*, and other assorted firearms and law enforcement related publications. My blog is at the Backwoods Home blog group.

It's backwoodshome.com/blogs/massadayoob, and for anyone interested in training, check out

MassadAyoobGroup.com.

Rob: And of course they can always tune into the Pro Arm Podcast.

Mas: Yeah, baby! I'm not a podcaster per se. I'm just one member of the podcast crew. The producer and editor, and therefore "prediter" is Gail Pepin. It's a group of eight or 10 of us who are all professionals in the field. We get together for roundtable discussions on different training topics or gun topics, and what I think is particularly useful, we have a number of interviews in the archives, and continue to do those, with people who have been in gun fights and survived and share what were the salient points of their survival, their experience in hopes that other people can benefit if they're ever in the same place. Go to proarmspodcast.com, and I believe all of the 70 or so that we've done thus far are available at no charge to download on computer or iPod.

Rob: Sounds good. Thanks again for coming on the show here.

Mas: Thank you, Rob, for all that you do.

Selecting and Using a Knife as a Defensive Tool

Michael Janich has been studying and teaching self-defense and the martial arts for more than 30 years. He has earned instructor's credentials in American Self-Protection (ASP – an eclectic art that includes elements of judo, aikido, boxing, fencing and French Savate), the Filipino art of Serrada Eskrima, and Joseph Simonet's Silat Concepts and is a member of the elite International Close-Combat Instructors' Association. He has also trained extensively in wing chun gung fu, tae kwon do, wu ying tao, Thai boxing, arnis de mano and military combatives. Janich is also one of the foremost modern authorities on handgun point shooting and is one of the few contemporary instructors to have been personally trained by the late close-combat legend Colonel Rex Applegate.

Rob: We're going to talk about selecting an everyday carry knife for use as a defensive tool. Can you tell us a little bit about your training, what you do, and your experience in this area?

Michael: I've been involved in the martial arts for about 35 years. I started training when I was about 12 or 13 years old. When I first got involved in the martial arts, one of the things that scared me the most was dealing with somebody armed with a knife. The art that I was studying at the time, American

Self Protection, and the techniques that we were learning didn't fare very well when we tried to do them with any type of realism. I went to my instructor and I asked him, "Hey, why do our counter-knife techniques suck?" and he gave me a bit of advice that I've always remembered and has guided my training ever since: "If you want to learn how to defend against a weapon, first learn how to use the weapon. That's the only way to understand its capabilities, its attributes, and its limitations."

That fueled my interest in studying the knife as both an offensive and defensive weapon, and it's something that I've pursued ever since. I've studied a variety of different systems, both formally and informally. I spent a lot of time training in the Filipino martial arts. Ultimately, I took the proven elements of the Filipino martial arts and wanted to adapt them to modern self-defense needs. When you look at knife tactics as they're applied in the Philippines, they're based on the culture and legalities of the Philippines and when you translate that into Western culture, it doesn't cross over very well.

So I tried to look at taking proven techniques, proven patterns in motion, proven methods, and adapting those to modern needs. The result is what I called Martial Blade Concepts, a modern personal defense system that focuses very heavily on the use of knives, but it does so in a way that is legally responsible and consistent with modern self-defense.

Rob: When you started training in martial arts, what was your goal originally?

Michael: This is early 1970s, so it was the Bruce Lee era. There were a lot of different reasons to train in the martial arts, but my primary motivation was self-defense. I grew up in the Chicago area. I was literally half a block outside of the

South Side of Chicago, so just barely in the suburbs. It was a grungy, blue collar area, not a super tough place to grow up, but getting in fights was not an unusual thing. There was also a spillover of crime from the South Side of Chicago into our area. We ended up moving out of there after there was an armed robbery down the block where two of our friends were shot and very seriously injured. Self-defense was the primary motivation. I enjoyed it for the athletic and fitness aspects, but really self-defense was always the core of my interest.

Rob: And like you said, there are several different reasons that you can do this, and a lot of people will go into it with the sport mindset. They want the camaraderie that comes with it and they want the fitness aspect of it, but if you're actually going into it for self-defense, you really have to take a different approach.

Michael: That's very true. As you said, there are many different reasons to train in the martial arts. You can do it from, again, a fitness aspect. You can do it from a cross-cultural aspect. You can get into it for competition and sport, but one of the things that's interesting about the martial arts is the term itself: "martial art." When you do the martial arts for other reasons, you have made the art more important than the practitioner, and in many cases, more important than the original goal.

As soon as the institution becomes the primary concern versus the individual's capabilities, you've gone astray when it comes to self-defense. That's one of the things that a lot of people misunderstand. For example, you take two people who walk into a Taekwondo school. Taekwondo happens to be a good example because it emphasizes kicking. If you have somebody who's six feet tall, reasonably trim, athletic, and flexible, they're going to excel at Taekwondo. They're going to do great. If you have somebody who has more of a wrestler's build, they're 5'2", stocky, short limbs. Taekwondo is not the appropriate sport or martial art for that person because the way that the techniques are presented, the emphasis of that particular art, doesn't lend itself well to that person's physical attributes.

When you look at teaching each of those people to fight, you have to choose tactics that are appropriate. There will always be some crossover as far as physical skill because we only have two arms and two legs. We only move in so many different ways, but ultimately a shorter, stockier guy is going to fight differently then a taller, leaner guy, and that's the way it should be. To make the art more important, and say the short stocky guy should learn how to kick above his head, doesn't make sense.

Rob: Any skill or knowledge that you have is only as good as its application.

Michael: It's only as good as its application, and ultimately, we're all inherently lazy. We tend to do things because they're not only effective but also because they're efficient. If you say, "This is the path of least resistance. This is something that is going to give me achievable results with the least amount of effort or the least amount of challenge," then you're going to be more efficient in what you do.

Rather then kicking somebody in the head, knock them down on the ground and stomp on his head. Bring the target to your feet versus bringing your feet to the target. That is a more efficient way to achieve that goal. When the art becomes more important then the practitioner and the practitioner's needs, then you are emphasizing the cultural aspect of it versus following the shortest path to self-defense.

Rob: When you realized that you were going after the self-defense aspect of it, you started looking at this in a different way. You started examining what the realities of the application would be. When you did that, you became interested in these edged weapons. Where'd you go from there?

Michael: I went into the Army at age 17, straight out of high school. I had been carrying a knife for several years and training with what I thought I knew at that point regarding knife tactics. I had a few like-minded folks that I trained with when I first got involved in the martial arts. We would do knife sparring and training based on the books that were available at that time. We pored through a lot of the classic World War II stuff and tried to make that stuff work. That was the time when Michael Echanis' works came out, the infamous black book that he had written. We gave that a try. We tried everything that we could based on what was available at that time, and we had a crude skill set.

In the Army I got to train with people from all different martial arts. It was a really great, eclectic training experience because you didn't have a lot of the political baggage that typically went along with the traditional training methodology. I got to cross train with people who did Filipino Sikaran, Kempo, Taekwondo, Aikido, Muay Thai, and Wing Chun, a bunch of different stuff. In the process, I maintained that interest in knife and tried to get other people interested in it, but it really wasn't until I found and tried to get into the Filipino martial arts that I discovered what I believe is really the most practical application of the knife.

I like to categorize their martial art as more of a tribal art. If you consider the history of the Philippines, you have a very disjointed culture. I don't mean that in a negative way, but because of the geography of the Philippines, you have so many different islands and so many different languages. In many cases you have elements of society that are separated from each other and because they are different cultures and there was no way to get everybody on the same page, but the thing that united them most was dealing with some type of foreign aggressor.

When the Spaniards came in and invaded the Philippines, defending against a foreign aggressor brought them together and gave them a common goal and purpose. In doing so, they looked at the fighting arts and their limited resources in a very practical sense. If somebody had a stick, you would teach him about the angles of motion, "You're going to take the stick and you're going to hit bony parts of the other guy's body and try to break bones." If somebody had a knife, you would say, "You're going to use those same angles of motion, so you have common technique, and you're going to cut fleshy parts of the body. You can cause damage that way."

If you had a big, sharp weapon like a bolo or a barong, then you had the ability to do both. You could cut, but you also had enough mass behind the weapon to be able to crush and break things. It was all designed to be very, very practical in the way that they applied the technique.

I'm not a big fan of sparring. I appreciate that the fact that people enjoy that type of thing as a sport or an athletic endeavor, but when you look at really being able to fight effectively with a knife, if somebody else is swinging a weapon at you, your first concern is his ability to hang onto his weapon.

If you can take the weapon out of his hand, then your life gets a whole lot easier. Your first target should be the hand that he extends toward you. It's not only the most available target, but it's also your first targeting priority. The Filipinos would "defang the snake", essentially cutting the mechanical structure of the forearm and hand, the muscles and tendons that allow the hand to grasp a weapon, and essentially take the weapon out of the fight. That's what's going to keep them safer sooner and give them a tactical advantage if it is a true warfare situation. By taking that concept to its natural conclusion, you end up essentially crippling the opponent. Then, if necessary or if you choose to, you can follow through and applying lethal force, depending upon the nature of the situation.

It's just like thinking strategically from a military perspective. If we're going to do an air strike, we want take out the antiaircraft capabilities of our enemy first. If we can do that with unmanned missiles and cripple their ability to shoot at our aircraft, that would be the first tactic that we would want to use. It just is the most sensible way to proceed, and the Filipino arts are very good at that.

Rob: It sounds like the reason the Filipino arts are so good is because they've thought this through in a practical, realistic manner.

Michael: Yes, they look at things pragmatically. Cheating is almost the governing factor of many of their tactics. Even in unarmed fighting, if you think of two guys getting ready to square off and fight empty handed, what you'll see from kind of a Western, Marquis of Queensbury rules type of thing is both people are throwing punches and trying to hit the other person in the head or the body. From a Filipino martial arts' perspective, they would first punch the other guy in the hands and fingers, and essentially break his hands to take away his ability to use his hands. Now those weapons have been eliminated. It's extremely practical, it's extremely smart, and it's the shortest route toward practical self-defense.

Rob: Let's move this over into our civilian world. Most of our listeners are in the US. So they're obviously dealing with a slightly different situation or set of circumstances then these people were when they were developing their sport, but they still need to take a realistic, practical look at where they would use these weapons, how they would use them, and see what tactics would work for them.

Michael: Exactly, and when you consider it in the context of modern self-defense, the same tactics actually become even more practical. If you're using a knife in personal defense, that means you're defending against some other type of contact distance weapon. You are in this situation for whatever reason. Your awareness, your avoidance, your ability to avoid the situation altogether was denied. You've been cornered in a confined area where you aren't able to escape and avoid.

Now you're facing somebody. That person has a contact distance weapon. You decide you're going to deploy a knife because you're forced to defend yourself. The first thing that that person is going to do, if they're really attacking you, is swing their weapon at you. This gives you access to the best target you could possibly hope for, the structure that allows that person to hold onto the weapon, essentially the inside of the forearm, the wrist, the flexor tendons, and the muscles of the forearm.

In simple anatomical terms, the muscles of the forearm contract to pull on tendons. The tendons make the fingers close, and that's what allows the attacker to grab and hold onto a weapon. He extends that toward you. Your first action is to simply cut the flexor tendons or cut the muscles deeply enough to disable that limb. You take away the function of the closing of the hand, and that will ideally disarm him. It's not only the most practical thing to do, but also, from a self-defense standpoint, it gives you stopping power.

The shooters out there are all familiar with the term stopping power. It's the ability to apply a tactic that will stop your attacker from endangering you. It's very different from the application of lethal force. Killing someone does not equate to stopping them in a practical and effective way. If you actually apply lethal force effectively, they will stop when they die, but in the process or in the time that it takes for them to die, they can still do serious damage to you and potentially kill you as well. You want is to emphasize stopping power over killing power, and you also want to do it in a way that is legally defensible. What the Filipinos would call "defanging the snake" is the ideal way to do that.

Rob: You're looking at taking away their ability to actually do you harm.

Michael: Exactly. If you were in a situation where you were being attacked and you could magically make the other guy drop his weapon, wouldn't that be your first choice? The magic is in crippling that hand. As soon as he extends it toward you, that's the primary target. You want to cut that and take away that physical action. This also emphasizes understanding human anatomy.

A lot of my research on the targeting methods that I use in Martial Blade Concepts was not based on talking to other martial artists or talking to people who have inherited martial traditions. Certainly there is a lot of good information there, but a lot of the validation that I've done is through talking to physical therapists, trauma surgeons, and people in the medical field and doing lots of medical research so that we can actually understand how the body works and how to make it stop working with a knife that we can legally carry.

Rob: So let's talk about the blade itself. What helps you to achieve these goals?

Michael: When a lot of people think about knife tactics, they're thrust focused. They say that a thrust is going to be more lethal than a cut and that should be the priority. This goes back to a lot of older martial tradition. Think about the metallurgy that existed hundreds of years ago. You didn't have really good metallurgy that would give you super sharp cutting edges that would hold an edge for a long time. Also when you look at medical knowledge and medical care from that era, if you were cut, the idea of being stitched up and treating a cut was something that was achievable at that time. You'd probably still survive. Because they lacked modern surgery and medical services, the deep thrust was more difficult to survive.

Thrusts were emphasized over cuts because they were more lethal. From a modern self-defense perspective, we've got a couple of things we need to think about. First, think about what you can actually legally carry. This is where, along with myths and misconceptions, you also have all the clichés that people will typically throw out. Typically at this point you'll hear, "I'd rather be tried by twelve than carried by six." Bottom line is: We're the good guys, and you have to try to play by the rules as much as possible.

Here in Colorado, according to the law, I can carry up to a three and a half inch blade. I want to play by the rules, especially given my reputation as a tactical trainer. A three and a half inch blade is, by definition, the tool that I will be allowed to use. I need to figure out what I can do with a three and a half inch blade that will allow me to effectively stop an attacker. I've found that the most effective way to do that is by cutting the body parts that allow him to be dangerous to me, essentially taking that concept of defanging the snake, biomechanically deactivating the bad guy, to even higher levels. We go beyond the idea of just targeting the grip. We also look at other targeting priorities, specifically bicep, triceps, and the quadriceps muscle at the front of the thigh.

Rob: You talked about going for the body and the head when you're fighting. This whole thrusting concept almost lends itself towards that mindset also, where you have to get at the torso, a target that's further away. Slicing and taking away the ability of the opponent to hurt you is an easier target of opportunity.

Michael: It's not only easier, but it is also going to produce results much more quickly and predictably. I wrote my first book on knife tactics back in 1992. It's called *Knife Fighting, A Practical Course*. I wrote it based on what I thought I knew at that time, which was basically a collection of both World War II era knife fighting stuff, traditional Western methods, and what I knew of the Filipino arts at that time. I got a call one day while I was working at Paladin Press in charge of their video department.

The call was from a guy who had been arrested for first degree murder. He explained how the situation had actually unfolded. He was working for a company that was bought out by a French company. His boss was doing some underhanded things. This man, the defendant, happened to speak French and the French company asked him to translate. He became a focus of a lot of the transitional aspects of the takeover. His boss felt that his life was falling apart because this employee was working with the new owners. The boss invited the employee over to his house. Employee walked in and the boss attacked him with a knife. The employee was able to reflexively deflect the knife and made the boss drop it. The boss grabbed him by the throat, threw him down on the ground, and started choking him to death.

The employee reached over and grabbed the knife, which happened to be a fixed blade SOG government model with about a six inch blade, and started stabbing his boss. The boss continued to choke him and moved from a choke with two hands to a choke with his forearm. The stab wounds moved over a little bit because he was now able to wrap his arm around the body. According to people in the neighboring apartments, they heard the fight go on for approximately five minutes. They fought through every room in the apartment and continued to fight until the cumulative effect of over 50 stab wounds finally made the boss bleed out. I became an expert consultant for this case to recreate the events and to help this guy in his defense.

He was ultimately acquitted of first degree murder and it was judged to be self-defense. During the case, I looked at the coroner's report and I saw multiple stab wounds that were judged to be potentially fatal. There were a number of wounds that by themselves should have killed this guy, and would have in time, but he still fought tooth and nail for five minutes. Five minutes is an eternity. Imagine if he still had a weapon. It's a very inefficient way to go. Look at the guy; even though this was a six inch bladed knife, this was a big guy. He was over 200 pounds. He was pretty portly.

When you consider a knife with a three and a half inch blade that can be legally carried in most places in the US, it's going to have a very different effect on 125 pound crack head versus a 250 pound biker. With somebody who has a very large physical structure, if you start stabbing him in the torso, you may not get to any vital organs with a small, legally carried blade, but when you look at the relative size of the limbs, the arms and the legs, there's not that much difference. The ability to effectively target them with a three and a half inch blade is much easier and it's going to produce more immediate results.

Rob: Cutting apart the structure that supports the weapon that's attacking you is very much more effective. Let's look at finding a tool that is most effective in this most effective tactic.

Michael: The first criteria that we're looking at is the laws in the your local area because you want to play by the rules if at all possible. For example, here in the US, you look at your state revised statutes and figure out what restrictions there are as far as blade length. Typically, you're also going to find any restrictions as far as like double-edged blades or something of that nature. I always recommend a single-edged blade if you travel frequently. Even if you're legal in your area, when you travel to some other location, you have to start the process all over again. Sticking with a single-edged blade is typically the best way to go.

Once you've got an idea of blade length, you want to look at blade design and function. You don't have to get too sophisticated here. A lot of people try to get into the minutia of "Well, this blade is better then this blade, and this configuration does this and this and this..." Bottom line is, with a three inch blade, you just need to have good edge geometry. This means that you've got bevels that come down to an acute cutting edge that will cut very efficiently and very effectively with very little drag, and you've got a good, sharp, usable point that is going to penetrate. It doesn't have to be anything super sophisticated.

I typically recommend staying away from tanto blades and anything that has a lot of belly to the blade. Think of your arm in motion. You're going to be moving your arm in an arc. That means the knife itself is going to be moving in an arc, and anything as far as the profile of the edge that would run parallel to the arc of motion of your arm means that you're limiting your cutting ability. Imagine a blade that has lots of belly to it, or an Americanized tanto blade. The tanto is an excellent illustration of this because typically you'll have is a straight cutting edge that transitions into the facet tip (the so-called armor piercing tip).

If your arm is moving in an arc, when you make contact, if you make contact at the very base of the blade, the heel of the blade closest to the handle, you're going to be cutting with full force because you have a straight cutting edge. You continue to press with full force, and you're maintaining that force until you hit that point where the tip is faceted. At that point, the tip rises very rapidly and that rise runs almost parallel to the arc of motion of your arm. When it does, you're no longer applying any pressure into the target. You're not cutting any deeper. You're not cutting any more efficiently.

You're burning calories and you're not making the wound any deeper. That type of point is extremely strong. If strength is something from a utilitarian standpoint that your use of the knife requires, that's fine, but when it comes to actually being able to puncture things, the more acute the point is, the more easily it's going to puncture. That's something that's been validated in actual medical tests that they've done on human cadavers to test different point profiles to see which one penetrates best. Having something that is going to give you both a sharp point and a cutting edge that is reasonably straight or has a just a small arc to it is going to be your best bet.

Rob: Having a straight edge allows you to get the most effective cut with that three and a half inches of blade?

Michael: From a practical standpoint, yes. Some people will argue that. They'll say that a curved edge has more cutting edge for a given linear blade length, but that last part of the cutting edge, unless you're actually able to apply significant pressure, is almost useless. It becomes a wrist snap to try to make that happen, and that's not something that you're going to do very well when you're in fear for your life and gross motor skills are overruling finer complex motor skills. If you think of most utility knives that you would buy to cut carpet or sheetrock, what is the blade shape? It's a Wharncliffe. It's a straight cutting edge that allows you to cut with full power all the way to the point. In a short blade, that is going to be the most efficient cutting tool that you can possibly have.

Rob: We're looking for something that's going to have a good grind, that's going to allow you to cut effectively, a relatively straight edge, and a pointed tip. We're talking specifically about a defensive tool, so we're not trying to balance this with utility or anything else. We're just talking about what you are looking for in a defensive tool. If you want to blend this into something else, you can work with that later. Take and blend these different characteristics into whatever else you're looking for in a knife, but that's what you're starting out with for a defensive tool.

Michael: Some people may look at the Wharncliffe design and say that the point is maybe too fragile for their tastes. Okay, great. Choose something that has a little bit of a curve to the edge. That brings the edge up into the thicker portion of the blade. It's going to give you a little bit more point strength. If that is something that you prefer, that's great, just don't take it to the point to where you have such a sweeping curve or so much belly to the edge that we're back into that situation where you can't apply pressure to cut with full power all the way to the point.

There are many fans of hawkbill blades or Karambit style blades. The Wharncliffe gives you, in my opinion, the same cutting aggressiveness that you would have with the Hawkbill, which works like the claw of an animal or the beak of a bird. It wants to grab and collect material and pull it into the shallowest part of that curve. The Wharncliffe gives you that same aggressiveness, but without the danger of potentially hooking onto things that you don't want to get snagged on.

If you were to cut the forearm with a hawkbill in such a way that the point went between the radius and ulna, you've snagged onto the limb and you can't finish the cut cleanly without having to severely articulate your wrist. The hawkbill can cut very, very well, but when you start mixing bones and other materials into the potential targeting mix, it can also become a hook and get snagged when you don't want it to. I feel that the Wharncliffe is the best compromise. It still gives you a very aggressive cut to the tip without becoming a fishhook.

Rob: So if the tip sweeps up, you lose a little bit of cutting power on the ends of your stroke. If the tip sweeps down, you can potentially catch on things, which will actually stop your stroke and hold you up there. The Wharncliffe is right in the middle of those two, and in your opinion, is the best compromise.

Michael: In most cases, the next consideration will be choosing either fixed blade or folder, but most people, from a practical and a legal standpoint, are going to be carrying a folding knife. You want to look at strength. You're looking at overall structural strength. You're also looking at the lock strength and lock design. Make sure that you have something that is going to be up to the rigors of full-force cutting on an attacker. In addition to strength, you need something that is not prone to accidental release.

A lot of people will argue locks in a general sense and they'll say that this lock is better than that lock, is better then that lock. In my opinion, there are three elements to any knife. You have the actual design, the engineering, and the execution of the engineering. If you screw up any one of those, you can still produce something that is not up to the task. You can have the greatest design in the world, but if it's poorly engineered and the stresses are not well managed, it's not going to work well. On the other hand, it could be designed really well, engineered really well, and then poorly executed, and it's still going to fail. What you want is something that you can trust, something that is going to be up to the task as far as lock strength and overall structural strength, because it has to be able to absorb the impact of full powered cuts.

The next element that you need to look at is handle design. Handle design needs to not only be ergonomic and feel good in your hand, but it also needs to allow you get a proper grip with good traction and a good texture without being so aggressive that it poses a danger to your own hand. You have to look at shock management. When you cut full power with a knife, that shock is transferred back to your hand. If there are any aspects of the knife that are so aggressive, or so pointed, or so sharply textured that it ends up tearing up your own hand, you may end up disarming yourself. Proper handle design is also an important consideration.

Next up would be carry method. Typically the pocket clip is the way to go. I started carrying knives back in the '70s. At that time, what we now take for granted as the so-called "tactical folding knife" didn't exist. I was carrying a Gerber Folding Sportsman 2. It didn't have a pocket clip. It didn't have a purpose designed one-hand opener. I bought something for 5 bucks called a "Flick-It". You would actually slide it onto the back of the blade to give you a thumb purchase, so you could thumb it open one-handed.

Around 1980, Spyderco defined the modern tactical folding knife. They were the first company to put out a purpose-designed one-hand manual opener via the Sypderco hole. They were the first company to put a clip on a folding knife. They were also the first company to put serrations on a folding knife. All three of those things were incorporated into their very first product, and essentially defined what we now take for granted as the modern tactical folder. The clip is still the most efficient way to carry the knife, not only conveniently but in a way that is immediately accessible for a quick draw.

Rob: When you first started talking about the structural strength, I wanted to hear you talk about fixed blades. They are so simple and almost sound like the best choice, at least in those first respects.

Michael: If you live in an area where you can carry a fixed blade, obviously that is a great go-to choice. I travel a lot for work and for training. Here in Colorado, I can carry up to a three and a half inch fixed blade. If I carry it in a way that is openly visible, it's going to raise some eyebrows. Unless you live out in a rural area where openly carrying a fixed blades is something that is accepted, it's going to be something that is more hassle than what it's worth.

A fixed blade is obviously going to offer you the greatest strength you can possibly hope for. It's also easier and faster to deploy if it's carried in a way where the handle is immediately accessible (either partially concealed under an over garment or carried openly). When you carry it deeply concealed, things slow down considerably. Even traditional neck knives can sometimes be slower to get into action than a folder carried in your pocket. I'm not dismissing fixed blades by any means. In a perfect world where we could carry whatever we wanted, a fixed blade would be the go-to choice, but from a practical standpoint, from a legal standpoint, and certainly my personal standpoint because of my travel, the folder is my first choice.

Rob: So you've found that when you compare the advantages of a fixed blade, the strength and the speed of deployment, you found that those are not that much greater than in a folding blade, and that's not enough to overcome the hassle that it is for you?

Michael: It's a personal choice based on my lifestyle and the fact that I do have to travel frequently. If I were to focus on carrying a fixed blade because I live here in Colorado, that means that my training should revolve around the use of the fixed blade because I need to support my weapon choice with proper training and proper tactics. The problem comes as soon as I hop on a plane and I fly someplace else where they have different laws. I can't carry a fixed blade anymore. Now the training that I've done has ingrained skills and habits that force me to go back to a weapon that I can't carry in that area.

I would either have to carry illegally or I change gears every time I travel. In 2012 it's looking like I'm going to be traveling about 18 to 20 times. Every time I hop on a plane, I can't change gears and mentally switch from fixed blade to folder just because I'm going someplace outside of Colorado.

Rob: So it sounds like it's a slight compromise for you, because of your lifestyle. You wanted to make sure that you can have one blade that you train on, and that you're most effective with. That decision is going to be different for everybody, but not much changes. You can still have these blade profiles with a fixed blade knife. You can still set it up very similarly. You brought up the fact that you want to have a knife that's going to be strong enough not to fall apart and be able to handle you putting a full stroke on it. Are most knives nowadays going to be able to handle that?

Michael: Most well-made knives.

Rob: Not out of your local gas station.

Michael: Exactly. If you buy a quality knife from just about any reputable manufacturer, you can trust it as a defensive weapon. All the major US manufacturers will offer something that is going to fall into that category. If you buy cheap, you get what you pay for. If you invest in quality, then you're going to have something you can trust with your life.

Rob: Let's talk quickly about ergonomics. You mentioned if the blade is strong and it gets caught on something, the next weakest point is the hand-to-knife interface. What are you looking for in that?

Michael: There are a lot of different schools of thought. When you understand anatomy and the Filipino approach to the use of small knives, you realize that the strength of your grip is actually in the last three fingers. A lot of people think that because we have opposable thumbs, the strength of the grip is between the index finger and the thumb. That certainly completes the grip, but it's not where the strength is. Think about shooting a handgun. You're going to hold onto the handgun very firmly with the middle finger, ring finger, and little finger of your hand. The thumb and index finger are free to operate separately. This is because they're on a different set of nerves and muscles.

The strength of the grip, which allows you to manage recoil, is in those last three fingers. In a small knife, you really want a little bit of a taper to the handle. When you think about the way your fingers are structured, your fingers get shorter when you go from the middle finger down to the pinky. As you close your hand, you're forming a bit of a cone. If you put a tapered object into that cone, everything locks into place, and you get lots of surface area, lots of contact, and you also have a very firm stop.

If you see still photos of Filipino martial artists doing their technique, in a lot of cases you'll see that their index finger and thumb are actually held somewhat loosely and the function of the grip is in those last three fingers. Based on that, you want a grip that a has a little bit of a taper to it, a good texture, and feels comfortable in your hand. A lot of people think you have to have finger grooves or some kind of a big choil that serves as a guard to keep your hand from sliding forward onto the blade. You keep your hand from moving forward onto the blade through a proper grip, not through guards.

With a small knife that doesn't have a guard on it, focus on the last three fingers of the hand. They are truly the strength of your grip because they are attached to a larger muscle group. Maybe you're thrusting. You're aiming for soft tissue but you happen to hit something hard like a belt buckle or bone. If your hand does slide slightly, the three fingers and palm are a nice, large, gripping surface area. Also, the padded portion of the palm near the knife edge of the hand is a much better shock absorber than just the index finger and the thumb. When you have a smaller surface area, and the hand does slide forward, there's really nothing to stop it. There's nothing to absorb that shock.

You want to look at the way the hand works. Going back to shooting a handgun, you want to dump all the forces of recoil into the meatiest portion of the hand. You want to make sure that you have the most surface area working for you as possible. There are a lot of people who like a pure, old hammer-grip. That's great. Just gripping the knife like a hammer in your fist is perfectly fine. The Filipino grip with the thumb on the back of the blade does give you better accuracy because it makes the knife a natural extension of your hand. Think about touching something with your thumb. Extending your thumb allows you to be very accurate without having to try very hard. If you simply grab the knife in your fist, you do have a very strong grip, but your level of accuracy, speed, and precision is reduced.

Rob: I also want to get your opinion on opening methods. I'm talking about either thumb studs, thumb holes, one-handed opening versus two, or even assisted opening or flippers. What do you find to be most effective?

Michael: I find the round, Spydercohole to be the most the most effective, practical, and elegant solution to being able to get a knife open quickly. It not only gives you more opening method options, but it's also a larger surface area to index. Under stress, gross motor skills take over. The idea of opening a folding knife is already, by nature, a somewhat complex motor skill, so the larger the index you have for your thumb, the better off you're going to be.

Thumb studs tend to be smaller and allow the knife to be slightly slimmer in the closed position. Part of getting leverage in opening a folding knife is the position of the purchase that you have for your thumb in relationship to the blade's pivot pin. Look at a closed folding knife with a thumb stud. The closer that thumb stud is to the centerline of the handle, where it's close to the pivot pin, the less leverage you have. If it's higher, above the pivot pin, when you push on it, the blade will pivot more easily because you have that extra offset.

With gross motor skills, driving your thumb straight forward is going to be a strong, simple motion. If that thumb stud is very close to the line of the pivot pin, when you drive forward you have to get it to pivot in an arc in order to open the blade. Without a decent offset between the lines of the pivot pin and the thumb stud, you can't really get that leverage. It's like you're trying to push the blade out of the end of the handle versus getting it to pivot. If the thumb stud were 90 degrees off from the pivot pin, pushing straight forward with your thumb, essentially parallel to the length of the handle, would move the blade right open. If you have that offset between the two, it allows the blade to pivot much more easily with a nearly straight thumb motion. Does that make sense?

Rob: Yes. The position of the thumb stud relative to the pivot is going to automatically make it easier. In other words, having the hole further out there, or having a stud set further out, is going to make opening easier.

Michael: Exactly. When you think of the flipper, you've got that flipper tab that is offset almost at a 90 degree angle from the pivot pin. You've got a good lateral separation between the two. When you pull on that flipper, it's going to open the blade very easily. It requires very little strength. The downside to the flipper is that you have to compromise your grip on the handle to be able to pull with your index finger to get the blade open. It causes you to shift your grip and you're going to have less skin on the handle when you do that. Under the duress of a defensive situation, the more tenuous your grip, the more likely you are to drop the knife or to screw up your opening. My preference for rapid deployment of folding knives, is to focus on inertial openings. There are knives out there that, because of their design, can be inertiallyopened by just about anybody. Those cases are a matter of poor detent or self-close to keep the blade in a closed position. A properly designed knife will stay closed until you apply proper technique to open it. An inertial opening allows you to draw the knife and get the blade open and into action very quickly without having to rely on any complex motor skills like thumbing the blade open. The trick to inertial openings is remembering that the blade is always going to pivot at the pivot pin and it has to be the center of the arc of motion to impart that inertia to the blade.

Rob: ...which should be practiced in advance so you would know that. Are you talking about opening the knife completely with inertia or are you talking about using that to aid in the opening, to make it an easier shove with your thumb?

Michael: When you look at the definition of inertia, it's the likelihood or the property of an object to either remain still or to remain in motion until some external force acts upon it. Think of a closed knife blade. To open it with inertia, you are accelerating the entire closed knife in an arc around the pivot pin then stopping the handle. The blade continues, because of its inertia, and opens all the way. It overcomes whatever detent or self-close spring tension you might have to keep the blade closed. It not only overcomes that, but it takes the blade completely to the open position. You never touch the blade with your thumb.

Rob: So you're saying not to even use the thumb stud or the thumb hole if possible?

Michael: Correct. That's going to be the fastest way with a traditional folding knife to be able to get the knife into action. The problem is, a lot of people will never invest the training time necessary to master that technique. They still need to have the best thumb opening method they can. Even the people who do invest the time need to have back-ups for everything. My first, go-to move is inertia. Second is thumb opening. Third is two-hand opening.

Rob: What are your thoughts on the Emerson Wave?

Michael: The Emerson Wave is going to be the quickest way to get the knife into action because it actually opens the knife as it clears the pocket. There are a couple of downsides that you need to take into consideration. First, you'll be buying a lot of pants. The Wave, it is hard on your pants pockets. If you train, practice, and draw your knife regularly, it does take its toll.

Rob: I know someone who puts patches on that one section of their pocket.

Michael: It's just the nature of the beast. You've got a piece of steel that is snagging on your pants. It's going to take its toll and you are going to wear out your clothing more quickly. It also forces you into a specific motion with your draw stroke. If you carry tip up, right side (back of the closed blade facing to your rear), that'll be a standard draw, coming to the back of your right pocket to come out into a standard grip. You have to use a rearward motion to draw and open the knife so that as it clears your pocket, the Wave snags and it opens in such a way that it clears your body and you don't accidentally get cut.

If you're forced to open the knife in confined quarters like if your back is against a wall, if you're caught between two cars, or any kind of confined quarters, the rearward motion is a downside. You have to think about making sure that you clear that path of motion before you go to draw your knife. If you instinctively go to draw the knife, grab it, pull backward, and drive your elbow into a brick wall or the side of a car, you can injure yourself or get to the point to where you just can't get your knife out because you have painted yourself into a corner with your draw stroke. It's a very quick way to get the knife into the fight, but it's also something that forces you into a specific pattern of motion and you have to make sure your body dynamics allow you to clear that range of motion before you deploy the knife.

Rob: Don't rely on that solely.

Michael: I believe that you need to have back-ups to everything. You still need to have some other type of opening option. Maybe it's the thousandth time that you draw out of those pants and you end up tearing your pocket and the blade doesn't open. Maybe you draw at a different angle and it doesn't snag properly. You need to make sure that you always have a back-up so if you don't hear that satisfying click, you're ready to do a thumb opening, a two-handed opening, or an inertial opening. You need to have somewhere to go from there.

Rob: Or all three of those.

Michael: Exactly.

Rob: Let's talk about training blades.

Michael: We've talked about a lot of the different criteria for selecting a knife. I get this question often: "I've X amount of dollars to spend on a knife. What should I buy?" My typical response is, "Find a good high quality knife that you can buy for 100 bucks that also has a matching trainer you can buy. Now you have something that you can use to train realistically so that you've got the skill to use the knife." Don't buy a $200 knife and forget about the skills to go with it. Make sure that you have a purpose designed trainer so that you can invest the time and effort in the proper training and have a skill set to use the knife correctly and efficiently.

Rob: There are several ways to do this. Nowadays there are a number of different manufacturers that also sell trainers. Is this a trend that you think is increasing? Is it on the rise?

Michael: It's not increasing as quickly as I would like it to. Certainly, there are a number of companies out there that do offer trainers. The problem with folding knife trainers is that the manufacturing process is just as expensive as it is for a live blade. You still have to make all the parts and heat-treat the parts. Well-made trainers typically use skeletonized blades. The holes take away metal to equalize the blade weight with an actual, live-blade version of the knife.

Rob: So you make it thicker at the edge, but you use holes to make it the same weight overall?

Michael: Exactly. Think of a live blade. You're grinding away steel to achieve that cutting edge. With a trainer, you're leaving the cutting edge at full thickness, but then you're taking holes out of the blade to remove steel and equalize the blade weight. When it comes to deploying the knife, you don't want a false sense of security because you have a big, heavy blade that you can open very easily. When you go to open the live blade knife, now you're working with a lighter blade that has less mass and less momentum, and you can't get it open. You need to make sure that you have that equalization of weight.

All those machining processes to produce the trainers are typically just as expensive as the live blade, and a lot of companies haven't embraced that. When I was with Blackhawk, it was very difficult to get them to make trainers. They only produced one trainer the entire time that I was there, and they didn't want to do it again.

Rob: If you think about it from their perspective, they know they're not going to sell nearly as many of the training models. From an economic standpoint, it's difficult for them to justify it.

Michael: Yeah, from a true business standpoint. The sad truth is that trainers are harder to sell because they're more expensive, and there just aren't enough people who invest the time in training to invest in those products.

Rob: What do you recommend for people that don't have a trainer available? What about modifying or trying to make something that they can practice with safely?

Michael: If you carry a folder, ultimately you want to have something that replicates your actual carry knife as closely as possible, but still allows you to train safely. You need to be able to combine all the elements of mitigating a threat empty handed, drawing the knife, opening the knife, and then applying the knife. You need to be able to put all those pieces together. The idea of representing a folding knife with a fixed blade trainer is not good enough in my opinion. Unfortunately, a lot of companies don't make training versions of every model they sell.

Some companies don't make trainers at all, and in those cases, I've personally made my own. I've also had students come up to me, show me their new knife, and say, "I just spent 150 bucks on this, and here's 150 bucks that I spent on a second one. Please take this to the grinder and turn it into a drone so I've got a safe trainer." Most knife edges can be ground down, rounded, and polished to achieve enough edge thickness to use as a safe training version.

Rob: Obviously, you're not going to be able to put material back onto the edge, so you're going to be shoving that edge back a little bit and change the cutting geometry just a little bit, but it's better than nothing.

Michael: There is another option that I've experimented with a little bit. If you go to a hobby shop, you can get some very small diameter brass tubing. You slit that tubing with a dremel tool. After you grind the sharp edge off the knife and round the tip, use JB weld to put this brass tubing onto the edge to actually thicken the edge. So it's still thin enough to be able to fold into the handle, but now you have a broader surface area that allows you to make safer contact with a partner.

Rob: Fantastic idea. Again, like you mentioned, make sure that you're still grinding away that edge in case it falls off or something happens to it.

Michael: Exactly right, and you also have to make sure to round the tip so that you don't have a sharpened point.

Rob: I appreciate you talking with us and giving us your insight. I think this is very helpful stuff.

Michael: Well, thank you very much for the opportunity. I appreciate it, Rob.

Thoughts on Knives as Defensive Tools

Dave Spaulding was awarded the 2010 Law Officer Trainer of the Year Award. He is a 30+ year Law Enforcement & Federal Security Contractor veteran. Dave was a founding member of his Agency's SWAT Team and performed hundreds of forced entries. He spent 12 years as its training officer. Dave spent five years as a full time use-of-force instructor, and another five years as the commander of a multi-jurisdictional drug task force working major narcotics cases from Seattle to Miami. He has worked in corrections, communications, patrol, evidence collection, investigations, undercover operations, training, and SWAT — and has authored more than 1,000 articles for various firearms and law enforcement periodicals. He's also the author of the best-selling books Defensive Living and Handgun Combatives.

Dave is also a graduate of most of the major shooting schools including Thunder Ranch, Gunsite, Mid-South Institute of Self-Defense Shooting, Smith & Wesson Academy, SIG-Arms Academy, Heckler & Koch International Training Division, Lethal Force Institute, Beretta Training Division, CQB Services, Ltd. and Defense Training International.

Rob: Let's talk about selecting a knife for personal defense and what to look for.

Dave: Why would you want to use a knife for personal defense, unless it was a last-ditch weapon? I bring this up because, like many people, I have been to a lot of the knife defense classes, or counter-knife classes, with some of the big-name instructors. I could not help but think while I was learning all these maneuvers that when two people willingly square off and start slashing at each other, the winner is merely the one that gets to go to the hospital! It's just like running into a blender. Why would you do that? Why would you stand there and deliberately trade slashes with each other?

If we take the Hollywood aspects out, and we're going to use the knife as a last-ditch backup weapon, or a weapon to get someone off of you, or something like that, I can wrap my head around that concept, but the idea that two people are going to square off and slash and jab is just so foreign to me. It's ill-advised. Anybody that's carrying a knife, looking for such a confrontation, is a fool at best and a crazy man at worst!

Rob: The reason that people carry a gun is not because they're looking for a confrontation, but in case something happens where it's required. Obviously a firearm is preferable to a knife in almost every case, but there are places where you may not be able to have a firearm and a knife is a good option.

Dave: And a knife is better than going open hands. I can get my head around that. It is a tool to repel an attack, but we're not going to square off and do this knife-duel. With that in mind, I agree. I've carried a knife since I was twelve. Back when I went to school, somebody carrying a Swiss Army knife in their pocket in school was not even thought of as foreign. Nowadays, you would go to jail. With that in mind, if you're going to carry a tool as a personal-security device to repel an attacker when a firearm is not available, the first thing that I would say is: "How often are you going to practice with it?" You might think: "What do you mean practice with it?" I'm talking about having the ability to get that knife out of your pocket, out of the sheath, and deploy it. I'm talking specifically about folding knives because that's what most people carry. They get a folding knife. They get the latest, greatest, CQB, ninja, Navy Seal, folding, serrated, Tanto, drop-point, spear-point blade, black-coated, and they stick it in their pocket and they think: "I'm ready to go!"

Understand that during times of high stress, or attack, you're going to lose digital dexterity. The blood, without any choice on your part, will leave those areas that the brain has determined are less important. It goes to the large muscle masses like the legs and the arms, to prepare for what's called "Fight or flight". Blood is not going to stay in the fingers. If you're thinking about getting your hand on a knife, pulling it out of your pocket, getting your thumb on the thumb-stud or in the hole on the blade, and getting it open, adjusting the knife to a saber grip, and then getting that perfect stance – all without extensive practice, so that you can perform that act without conscious thought, you're kidding yourself. If you haven't practiced to that point, you're going to reach into your pocket, and because you have no digital dexterity, you're going to pull the knife out, and you're probably going to fling it across the room.

With that in mind, if you're going to use a knife for that purpose, you're probably better-served with some sort of fixed blade.

Rob: So you're recommending a fixed blade?

Dave: Right. If you're not going to put the extensive practice into it, it'll be the same thing I tell cops if they're going to use that threat-level-three duty holster, where you've got to hit this button, hit that snap, rock that thing back, draw it up and out of the holster, and put it on the target. If you're not going to put extensive practice into that holster so that you can do that without conscious thought in a crisis, then get yourself a simpler holster! I don't carry in uniform-duty capacity anymore. I carry concealed, and my holster is nothing more than a Kydex scabbard because it's simpler to use. All I've got to do is clear my garment, acquire my grip, and draw. Same thing with my knife. If I'm going to carry a knife for personal security, it's probably going to be some sort of a small, fixed-blade knife that I can get my hands on easy, draw it, and go right to work.

I carry a folding knife, but I carry it as a cutting tool. I've long said that if you're in some sort of a job where you're required to carry a gun, or you feel like your life is such that it is advisable to carry a gun, then you probably should carry a knife too. You are in a high-threat environment. You may need the knife to do nothing more than to cut a piece of rope or a seat belt normally, but if you're in a potentially high-risk situation, having some sort of cutting tool would be to your advantage. I carry a folder for that purpose. Can I get the folder out and use it in a defensive situation? I can, but I have practiced with it a lot. I have practiced getting my folder out of my pocket the same way I have practiced drawing my pistol from the holster. If I was going into an environment where I could not carry a gun, and a knife was going to be my primary tool of security, it would be a small, fixed blade.

Rob: It's the same way with a firearm, the more you practice, the more likely it is that you're able to handle, under stress, highly dexterous tasks. When you talked about getting the gun out of some of those holsters, it sounds like some sort of video-game cheat combo, left-right-left-right-up-circle, whatever.

Dave: Right.

Rob: Some of these kids -- I'm not a video gamer but I've watched some of my cousins go at these things -- can memorize and work these things over and over so that it's just second nature to them. I want to offer up that with practice, nearly anything is possible.

Dave: Yes, with repetition. Somebody that says you can never get a folding knife out in a fight is incorrect. That's not true. There are documented cases where people have gotten folding knives out under duress. There are videos out there where you'll see a guy deploy a folding knife, but usually he uses two hands like he's opening his Case Triple XXX pocketknife. There also have been situations where highly skilled people have been able to draw a folding knife from their pocket and get it open with the same hand.

Kelly McCann, the founder of Crucible, told me a really interesting story about one of the guys he had worked with. The guy had been overseas working a security detail. He stopped in a European country where guns are pretty much banned. It was an R&R thing before he came back to the United States. He and a buddy were coming out of a bar when, out of the clear blue, he was accosted by a guy with a big knife. This fellow reported that, without thinking, he reached into his hip pocket, got his folder out, opened it up, and stuck it into the guy's neck, and he couldn't remember doing it.

That's unconscious competence. You hear police officers and armed citizens and protective agents give you debriefs: "The gun was in my hand, I don't even remember drawing it." The same thing can be done with a knife, but again, it takes repetition. If you're not willing to commit to that level of practice, then simplify it by using a fixed blade. You'll just make it easier on yourself.

Rob: So let's talk about the carry and deployment of a fixed blade. Where do you think is the most efficient place to carry it?

Dave: It depends on what you're doing. If you're used to carrying a pistol on your strong side at your waistband, and you're going to some country where you can't carry your gun, but you can carry a knife, it would make sense to carry your fixed blade inside the waistband on your strong side where your pistol would normally be. You've already got an anchored motor skill that will allow your hand to clear the garment and go to that area.

However, if you're carrying a handgun and don't want to tie up that gun hand with the knife, it might be a good idea to have that fixed blade on your off-side. Maybe behind your spare magazine. If you think about it, you've probably practiced bringing that left hand --or that right hand, whichever one is your off hand-- back to grab that magazine to insert it in the gun. That same motor skill can be applied, just traveling a little further past that magazine on your waistband to your knife.

Where you carry it is going to depend on the situation. It's going to depend on what type of equipment you've already got around your waist. It will depend on lots of things. There's something to be said for carrying a very small fixed blade in the change pocket, or what some people call the watch pocket, on your blue jeans, just forward of your hip. You should experiment to determine what really works best for you.

Rob: You mentioned going to a place where your gun may not be legal, but your knife is. An interesting thing that

I've found is that in most places, overseas especially, where you're not legally able to carry a gun, you also would not be able to carry most knives. Make sure that you double-check the laws, but remember that there are ways around a lot of overbearing laws. It may be just a certain knife length. It may be that a folding knife may be legal whereas other knives might not be.

Dave: Yeah, there are a lot of places where folding knives that don't lock open are legal. By the same token, in some places guns are seriously illegal. Someone carrying a small knife, and I'm not talking about a Rambo or a certified Bowie knife, that looks like a craft knife or X-acto blade is less likely to suffer the wrath of the local constabulary than if you had a semiautomatic pistol in a holster. Keep that stuff in mind. I've known a lot of guys that have gone overseas, and they've carried linoleum knives and things that look like tools. You've seen those curved blades on linoleum knives. I really don't want to come up against the wrong end of that. So there are ways to keep yourself armed in areas where that kind of stuff is frowned upon.

Rob: A knife is also much easier to conceal then a firearm.

Dave: Sure, absolutely. How would you like to come up against somebody that's got about a 2-foot long screwdriver with a sharpened end?

Rob: I think I'd pass.

Dave: Yeah, me too. There are lots of things that can be considered edged weapons that are not knives. It's up to your imagination. There's no reason to be unarmed if you have trained yourself to look for things that can be weapons.

Rob: You're talking about Jackie Chan-style. Use whatever you can, the shopping cart, the refrigerator, the bat lying in the street.

Dave: I repelled an attack one time with a rolled-up magazine.

Rob: Whatever works.

Dave: You roll up a magazine and you can hold it in your hand like a club. It was stiff as a board, and the guy came at me. All I did was jab him in the chest and he fell down choking on the ground.

Rob: Maybe if your wife is not necessarily happy about you collecting all these different knives, you can say, "I need this knife for this specific law in this area, and I need this knife for this area, in case I have to travel there." So you have a good excuse to collect extra knives.

Dave: Again, if you're actually going to carry different knives, you had better make sure that they open alike, because you're going to be developing a motor skill to deploy that knife. You don't want to have this knife function this way, with a tip-down carry, and the next function this way, with a tip-up carry. You want to collect a battery of knives that carry alike and open alike.

Rob: Not only are you practicing grabbing something very different than a handgun, but ever knife is gripped slightly differently.

Dave: Right, same with any handgun. They all feel different.

Rob: The transition from a handgun to grabbing a knife that's in the same area is especially different. You mentioned earlier that if you're in an area where you're not able to carry the firearm, it's great to keep it on that strong side where you're used to moving your hand if something occurs. Sure, you are used to that, but you've also have to realize that that alone is not good enough. You need to practice getting the knife out because moving your hand there may be similar, but the handle on that knife is going to feel very different from the grip angle on your firearm.

Dave: Right. Unless, of course, you're carrying the TDI knife from K-Bar.

Rob: And how does that differ? Because it angles?

Dave: Well, the TDI knife stands for the Tactical Defense Institute. It's a shooting school in Southern Ohio founded John Benner, who had the idea that if you developed a knife that had a bend in it, like a pistol grip, you could use the same motor skill to draw the knife that you use with a handgun. John intended this knife to be used primarily for weapon-retention situations. John envisioned the knife being worn by uniformed police officers on their inner belt underneath their duty belt, maybe behind their magazine pouches, so it was a low profile.

If somebody comes up and grabs your gun, your gun hand comes down to try to block it while your support hand reaches down and grabs this knife, which is shaped just like a pistol. You draw it straight up and out of the holster and you can start slashing and jabbing and going to work on somebody. That's going to repel an attack very quickly. It's been used four times that I know of, each time, very successfully. The knife has become very popular for just a carry knife because there are different sizes. You can get big, you can get small, you can get serrated, you can get drop point, whatever you want.

The bend makes it very easy to carry and very fast to bring into action. The nice thing about the TDI knife is that it's not very expensive. So if it gets left behind somewhere, or in someone, you don't feel like you've left your wallet behind as well.

I have a good friend, Ernest Emerson. He makes very nice, very high-end knives. A friend and I were on the range one time, and he had an Emerson Karambit, and he lost it.

Rob: Ow.

Dave: He was crushed, because this was a $250 knife. If a piece of equipment is so costly that you're going to feel like somebody's punched you in the gut if it gets left behind, then maybe we've spent too much money on it. I have nothing against Emerson knives. They are some of the best, but you've got to take that kind of thing into consideration when you're buying any kind of equipment, because a piece of gear that's used for combative applications can very easily be lost or left behind.

Rob: You mentioned earlier maybe having something with a small blade. What are your thoughts about the length of a blade that you'd use as a fighting knife?

Dave: I tend to like small knives. First of all, if you're trying to reach the vital organs, they may be only an inch or two deep, or they could be fairly deep, but in a knife fight, victory is usually achieved by stabbing and slashing the opponent enough so that he sees his life's blood leaking out on the ground, and he just backs off. The belief that you're going to penetrate deep enough to hit his heart and stop him, may be a little too optimistic about your ability.

You really don't need a very big knife. A knife with a blade that's about 3 inches long, is just big enough to fill my hand,

and I can get it open pretty easy. It should have a good-size thumb stud on it. I think that's pretty good. I don't feel like I need a knife that I can disassemble my pickup truck with. Some people will differ, and of course if you're getting ready to head to Afghanistan or Iraq, you may want a big, substantial knife. But for my lifestyle, my real world of work, I think a small, lightweight knife that's easy to pick up, with a 3-inch, blade is probably plenty.

If somebody reaches for me and all of a sudden I slash down on his inner forearm with it, I think he's going to notice.

Rob: I think there are a number of advantages that small blades have over large blades. The biggest thing is concealability. If you have a large blade, you can really give up that advantage.

Another advantage of smaller blades is the leverage. When you have a large blade, you can catch it on anything, a belt, metal, etc. Obviously, on some super-long blades are going to make a bigger difference, but it could be wrenched out of your hand, you could catch it on something. When you've got a smaller blade, you've got a lot more power, and the physics make it a better tool.

Dave: Yeah, I agree. Let's put the whole thing in perspective. You know what an Exacto knife is, right? A little craft knife?

Rob: Right.

Dave: As you know, it's got the stem, and you put the little blade in it, and what is it, three-quarters of an inch or an inch long?

Rob: Yes.

Dave: Take that and slash yourself across your forearm with it. Just visually slash it. Right there, you'd notice. How big a knife do you really need? Probably what you need is a knife that's sharp and that you can hang on to. You're going to do plenty of damage with something like that.

Rob: This is not a here's the best knife, go buy the K-Bar TDI. You're going to figure out what works for you. Just be sure that whatever blade you choose is sharp.

Dave: Yeah. When you buy a knife, you want to buy a sharpening accessory, whether it be a simple stone or an elaborate Lansky-type sharpener. Usually a few runs across the stone are enough to keep that thing sharp. If you let it go to the point where it's dull like a butter knife, now you've got yourself a real chore to keep that thing sharp. So it's like anything else. If you keep it sharp, if you maintain it, you can get the inexpensive Gerber knife at Gander Mountain and that knife will last the rest of your life.

Rob: What are your thoughts on serrated blades?

Dave: I like serrated blades, and it's because of my law-enforcement experience. Because I've cut lots of things. I had this conversation here just a few weeks ago with Rick Hinderer, who makes high-end knives for the tactical, the law-enforcement, and the military communities. We were talking about serrations, and I told him, "I like to have a blade that's got at least an inch or three-quarters of an inch of serrations, and it's because I sawed through things like rope and seat belts. I don't think you need an entire half blade or a full blade of serration, but having a small section back toward the hilt is good. A lot of times all you need to do is just saw just to get started, and then the regular straight blade will cut through.

I like to have a small section of serrations on my knives, and I've had the same conversation with Ernie Emerson, and he agrees. He says, "Knives are used far more often as cutting tools then they are used as weapons

Rob: The knife that I have on my hip right now does have a small section of serration on it. The only thing about serration is that it is a little bit of a pain to sharpen.

Dave: The serrations seem to hold their edge longer, and on some of those tough substances, they really cut well. But again, you don't need a lot.

Rob: Now, you mentioned that you carry a separate knife as a tool. Something different from your fighting knife, correct?

Dave: Right.

Rob: And that is something that I recommend for a lot of people because the one that you use as a tool, it is going to get dull. Get a little keychain knife. That's what I use to open packages, that's what I use to cut strings, plastic, or whatever I need. It works. And my larger folder is the one that I don't break out to open up the Christmas presents. That's the one that stays on my hip because I don't want to dull the blade; I don't want to have to take care of sharpening that as often.

Dave: Right, that works for you. I've had different models over the years. I tend to gravitate toward a 3-inch blade that has a thumb stud instead of a thumb hole. I always carry it tip up, and I carry it in my hip pocket on my strong side, right behind my holstered sidearm. I'm not advocating this to your listeners, but over the years, it's worked for me. Number one, my elbow goes straight to the rear, just like I'm going for my pistol, and then all I have to do is go past the pistol and insert my thumb into my pocket behind the body of the knife. I wrap my fingers around the clip, I pull it up, and as I'm pulling it up, I kind of cant it out so the stud on the knife blade catches the seam of the top of my pocket. So as I pull it out, the blade deploys. All I've got to do then is acquire a saber grip, and I'm ready to go. I've practiced that to the point where I can get it out quickly.

For me, that works very, very well, but then again, it takes a certain type of knife. It has to have a large stud on it so it'll catch the upper seam of the pocket. That works well for me, and I don't plan on changing it any time soon. I'm kind of like you. I use that for very serious purposes, and then I've got a little kind of a goofy knife that I use for cutting ribbon and opening letters and stuff like that.

Rob: I'm sure that whoever made that loves it being called a goofy knife, right?

Dave: I've had it forever. I don't carry it on a key ring. I kind of stick it in my pocket, but it's a little sheath knife and it's got a little dagger blade on it; I think it's a Techna knife, and I'm not even sure if they're made anymore. That's my knife that I opened up the lid for the Play-Doh for the kids.

Rob: One thing that I do want to bring up before we close this out. I want to make sure that if you're carrying a pocket folder knife, I really do recommend having a clip that will keep it at the top of your pocket. The right clip will keep it in place so you can know exactly where it is and grab it the same way every time.

Dave: I agree. I've never really liked the weight of a knife bottoming out in my trouser pocket, especially when you're wearing dress trousers. The nice thing about a pocket clip is whether you're wearing jeans, dress pants, whatever the case, you can lock it in so it's always where you need it to be. Like anything else, consistency is what will allow you to deploy it quickly.

Rob: Again, these are general things. Every person is different. Go find what works for you. Different clothing may require you to carry your knife in different ways. There are a whole slew of different factors. These are some general guidelines that should help you in selecting a knife that you can use to repel attacks.

Dave: In serious situations, again, using a blade is certainly better than going in open hands or fisticuffs with somebody, but I want to again caution your readers who may have some kind of a fantasy in their heads that they're going to pull out their knife and they're going to square off and do this Jim Bowie kind of slashing thing. Please don't! All you're going to do is get shredded.

Rob: If you've got that foolishness in mind, go back and listen to some of what we've talked about concerning the reality of self-defense. I think that most of our readers/listeners, are on the same page as you Dave.

Dave: You always run the risk of losing in any fight, but in a knife fight, once you've been sliced, diced and turned into julienne fries, that would be a really, really bad loss.

Rob: Yeah. Does anyone actually win a knife fight?

Dave: No. I don't think so. I don't know how you would because again, the one that wins probably is the one that goes to the hospital, not to the morgue.

Rob: The one that wins is the one who's lost the least blood or is still alive.

Knife Features and Recommendations

Dan is the Editor-in-Chief of bladereviews.com. He loves all kinds of blades, and has ever since he was a little kid. When he is not reviewing knives and harassing custom knifemakers, he is a full time graduate student in Florida. His hobbies include cycling, barbecue and fishing.

Rob: Today we're going to talk about considerations when selecting an everyday carry knife. This is something that a lot of people love to talk about. I'm sure we could spend hours discussing this, but I just want to hit on the major considerations. When you have decided to carry a knife where do you start? When you decide that you want to start carrying a knife, it's normally for a certain reason. Maybe you've gone to the post office too many times and said, "Man, I wish I had something to open my boxes or my letters," or maybe you were threatened and you wanted something as a defensive tool. That's where you'd start, right?

Dan: Absolutely. The first thing you want to do is consider what you're going to use this knife for.

Rob: What are some of the most common uses for an everyday carry knife?

Dan: I divide them in two categories. First, there are small, bare minimum type knives that you'd use for opening packages, mail, minor food prep, cutting string, etc. That would be something with a three inch or under blade. Then you have the larger knives that might flex into more of a personal defense kind of knife, but are still able to accomplish those utility tasks.

Rob: By nature, an everyday carry knife is going to be a blend of several different styles. It's not going to be perfect for one task unless you're sacrificing functionality in other areas. Because it's something that you have on you, you want to be able to use it for multiple tasks. You're going to have to balance it amongst the things that you're doing. If all you needed was a food prep knife, you'd pick up a kitchen knife. You could just leave that in the kitchen and use that. If all you needed was something to open up packages, you're looking at something very specific, but you want a knife that is going to be able to do a number of things well.

Dan: It's always a careful balancing act, and it's also a highly personal choice as to what really works for you.

Rob: We mentioned three specific things: Food prep, small cutting tasks like opening packages or those painful plastic clamshell containers, or a defensive tool. What sort of characteristics are we looking for when we refer to each of these aspects of use for an everyday carry knife?

Dan: First, make sure that you're going to be able to legally carry whatever you've decided. If you're looking for something that's going to be potentially used for your self-defense, you're going to want to make sure that there isn't some law in your city that says that you can't carry anything over three inches long. In my mind, that would be the first thing to consider. You're looking at stuff like cutting performance, blade shape is important. The type of grind that's applied to a knife is important. Blade steel may be important. There are a lot of things to consider.

Rob: Let's go back to the first thing you mentioned. Making sure it's legal is obviously very important. There are so many convoluted knife laws that, unfortunately, a lot of people just give up on it and say, "Whatever", and they open the door for themselves to get into a lot of trouble. You never know when you're going to be checked out by a police officer or someone who might make trouble for you. What have you found to be the best way to check into the knife laws and make sure that you're going to be good in your area?

Dan: My advice would be to contact perhaps your local authorities like a police department. You can also start looking on the internet for resources. There is a wealth of information at our fingertips. I don't have one particular source. I know for me, personally, what I can carry in Florida, but it's going to vary tremendously based on where you live.

Rob: Be careful that you don't just check with a state authority, because they can vary by town, county also. So if you're calling local authorities, make sure to check several different offices and kind of compare amongst them, see which is the most restrictive, go by those guidelines, and you'll be safe. Now that we've covered the actual legal aspects of it, let's move on to the knife itself. There are so many different variances amongst knives. There are so many different knives on the market, and then there are the custom knives. There have to be millions of different knife styles that have been made through history. It's just unbelievable, and there's a reason. There are different characteristics of knives that make them more or less suitable for different people and more or less suitable for different tasks.

let's talk about ergonomics. This is something that some people say is overrated and they don't care about that much. Other people swear by it. They wouldn't think of getting a knife that's not comfortable for them. Where does this fall on your scale? What are you looking for when it comes to ergonomics?

Dan: For me personally, ergonomics is a critical component when selecting the right knife. If it doesn't work in the hand for me, it's just not a knife that I'm going to use. It's incredibly important.

Rob: Ergonomics can involve the handle shape, size, weight, and even how it handles. Ergonomics is how it's going to handle in your hand. Even the blade shape can come into play in ergonomics, because it affects the way that you're going to hold the knife when you're actually performing the cutting tasks. All these things need to work together. Ergonomics for someone who's cutting tons of rope will be different from someone who is chopping apples or doing food preparation. You're going to have to look at how the handle fits. You're going to want to look at the shape of the blade and how that corresponds to what you want to use the knife for.

Dan: You're going to also want to look at the stuff like the texture of the handle to see if it has adequate grip. Look texturing on the thumb ramp and other parts where your fingers are going to be holding onto the knife. Yeah, it's important and there are a lot of factors.

Rob: The method of opening is also very important. The thumb studs may or may not work for some people. They may be uncomfortable and you may prefer the Spyderco holes. There is also assisted opening versus normal opening. There are a lot of different aspects that you have to choose from, and the simple fact is, there's not one that's better or worse than the other. It's about finding what works for you. What is going to make this a better tool? What is going to make this knife more useful? What is going to make it more enjoyable, comfortable, easier for you to use?

Dan: A lot of this stuff is just going to be personal preference. Try out multiple knives and settle on what works best for you.

Rob: If you have a buddy that has a lot of different types of knives, go over and play with his knives. Even if he doesn't have an exact model that you'll end up, you can at least check out the different characteristics and see how they feel and work for you. You'll try the different grip textures. You'll try the different opening methods. You'll try the different blade styles. Go down to your local gun store or knife shop. They'll probably have a decent selection of knives to check out. They may not let you cut with them and play with them as much, but at least you can get a good idea of several of the ergonomic aspects, and that's pretty important.

Dan: There is no real substitute for going to the store and physically picking it up and holding it and examining it to see how it really works for you.

Rob: Let's talk about the blade itself, arguably the most important part of the knife. This is the part of the tool that actually does the work. What are people looking for in a blade? The first thing I'm looking for in a blade is something that's sharp and actually cuts. I know it sounds simplistic, but there are some knives out there that are difficult to get sharp and sometimes don't come sharp. They're almost useless. I know every knife is for cutting and everyone's going to say that their knife is sharp. What are you looking for to make sure that you're going to have something that's actually going to cut?

Dan: You're going to want to start off with a quality blade steel, and there are many to choose from. That's a discussion within itself, but there are several. If the knife doesn't say what kind of steel it's made out of, that's typically a bad sign. If you're going to go with any kind of trusted brand, typically they're going to list the steel and you can do some research and determine if it's going to be good for you.

Rob: That's a great rule of thumb. There are so many steels out there that you're not going to know the characteristics of each one of them, but if it's unlisted it's probably not something you want. When it comes to steels, there's also a certain level above which you get into these super steels, and then the super -super steels. There is a cutoff point where it's more than most people need. Sure, if you're an enthusiast and you want to get into all the super steels, go for it, but if you're just looking for a tool, just an everyday carry thing, you don't need to get into that. Just make sure that you have a quality steel that's going to be able to get sharp and is going to last for a while. You also want it to be something that's not going to be rusting so badly that every week you have to polish the thing up to take the rust off of it. What else are you looking for in a good steel?

Dan: I think you covered most of the things I look for: ease of sharpening, edge retention, ability to resist rust and corrosion. You also want to look at the kind of coating or the finish on the steel, too. That's important because some finishes, like a sandblasted finish, are going to be making your steel a little more susceptible to rust than a coated finish or a stonewashed finish.

Rob: You talked about edge retention and ease of sharpening. Correct me if I'm wrong, but do these two oppose each other? When you have one that's good, the other doesn't work well, or can these two characteristics go hand in hand?

Dan: No, you're correct there because the softer a steel is, the easier it's going to be to sharpen. Unfortunately, the softer a steel is, the easier it's going to wear down and lose that sharpness. You are looking for a balance. The interesting thing with steels is that these two characteristics aren't necessarily inversely related because the different compositions, chemicals, and molecular structures can help to balance it in one way or the other.

Rob: Pick what you think is going to work well. If you're really good at sharpening your knives and you're comfortable taking the time to make sure it gets perfect, feel free to go for that harder steel, but if you're not very good at sharpening, or if you're not sure if you're good at it, try something a little softer at first, and work with that until you're better at it.

Dan: Yeah. I would say some good steels to start with, easy, forgiving, and inexpensive are AUS8 and HCR13MLV. Those are two steels commonly available in knives that are under $50, and they're quite easy to sharpen. Other steels have a little bit more of a learning curve and they will take more time to really put that razor edge on them.

Rob: Something else that's very important is the shape of the blade. When you're looking for a blade that can do multiple tasks, what kind of blade shape are you looking for?

Dan: For something that can do multiple tasks, I typically like something with a good amount of belly(the curvature to the cutting edge) because that enables you to really get the most out of however you're going to use the knife. A lot of that everyday usage is going to occur right on the belly, right where the curve is.

Rob: Without a belly, you're not going to have as much downward pressure in the middle of your cutting stroke. You can press down, but with a straight edge you're not going to be able to have all the pressure actually going into the object you are cutting. If you don't have that belly, a lot of times there will to be some stuff that's going to remain uncut if you're pressing up against a flat surface like a cutting board.

Dan: For a lot of EDC tasks, having some belly like that is quite nice , but that's not to really take away from a straight edged blade, referred to as a Wharncliffe style blade. Those are good too, but perhaps more for detail work and not necessarily for cutting against flat surfaces like you're describing.

Rob: There are other aspects of the blade besides just the sharpened edge of the blade. The spine/top of the blade varies quite a bit also. A lot of it's decorative, but there are so many different shapes and styles of the knife blade. The main consideration, at least in my opinion when you're coming to the rest of the blade, other than the edge, is the weight. If they put a nice swedge on it and keep it thin at the top, it's going to help cut down on the weight for you. Are there any other considerations when you're talking about blade shape, other then the edge?

Dan: You also want to take a look at the tip, especially if you're going to be using this knife for, self-defense or going to engage in a lot of kind of thrusting or stabbing type uses in your daily pattern of use of the knife. Having a strong tip can be very important for some people.

Rob: Another aspect that we haven't covered yet is the grind.

Dan: Yes, the grind is very important. You are going to find that most EDC knives are going to have one of two common grinds: a hollow grind(concave grind) or a flat grind(no curvature at all to the grind). Both of those, for all intents and purposes, can perform very well. Part of it will come down to personal preference in terms of which you like the look of. Flat grinds are generally considered to be better slicers, but hollow grinds are typically considered to be a little bit stronger, and I think they also reduce weight a little bit.

Rob: We also need to talk about the edge itself. Do you want a combination serrated/straight edge, just straight edge, or serrations? Again, a lot of this has to do with what you plan on using it for. Are you going to be cutting a lot of rope? Go for the serrated edges. That might be great for a fisherman or someone on a ship who has it for getting through the rope quickly if there's an emergency. My personal preference is a plain straight edge. What are your opinions on these three different types of edges?

Dan: I tend to agree with you. I like a nice, straight edge. If you keep this edge very sharp, it's going to cut just as well, if not better, than a serrated edge. Partially serrated edges can be handy though, especially if you're not going to be sharpening your knife that much. With a dull straight edge it's going to be difficult to cut through things, but you can saw through to get started with the serrated edge. If you have a specialized task for it, like cutting a lot of rope or maybe you're using it as a seatbelt cutter, you may want to consider that serrated edge, or partially serrated edge.

Rob: And there are even knives also where you can actually have a two separate blades, one full of serrations and the other a full straight edge. That might work well for situations like you mentioned. In my opinion, the straight edge opens up a lot more options for different tasks that you might encounter in everyday carry situations. That's what I'd recommend. It can cut through most things. If you want to have a serrated edge to quickly get through ropes and seatbelts, you might want to stash something in your car or on the boat near the area where you might need it. That might be an option for you.

Dan: Being prepared and knowing what kind of tasks you're going to run into is useful when you're picking out your knife, because most people probably aren't going to need to cut a bunch of rope every day.

Rob: The hardware on the knife is almost as important as the blade itself. How are you going to carry it? How are you going to have it near you? Are you going to carry it on a keychain, are you going to carry it on a clip, or are you going to use a lanyard? There are a number of different ways that you can carry a knife, and again, it's personal preference. You're going to have to figure out what works for you. Once you figure out what you want to do, you need to make sure that the knife gives you that option. A number of knives are only available with one carry configuration. Maybe the clip is only available on one side. Sometimes the clip can't be removed.

If you're a leftie and you're looking for something to carry on your left side and you want to be able to deploy it quickly, you want to make sure that the clip options allow that. If you want to take the clip off or put it on your keychain or carry it by a lanyard, you want to make sure that you have a good lanyard hole. You want to make sure that that clip is not embedded in the knife and you can't take it out. Are there any other carry considerations that people need to look at?

Dan: I typically enjoy carrying a knife with a pocket clip. That's become very popular, especially in the past decade or so. The pocket clip can be a conversation in itself because it's often a source of grief for a lot of people. It can be difficult to get the pocket clip right. You want to make sure you've got a clip that's has good retention, yet it's still not too difficult to get out of your pocket. You want to look for things like how the knife rides in your pocket. Is it comfortable? Is it bulging out of your pocket? Can people see that you're carrying some sort of large knife with you? There's a lot of stuff to consider, and it's all important because the way the knife interfaces with you in terms of your carry system is critical to you actually carrying the knife.

Rob: The clip design is very important. It can be a great clip that holds the knife exactly where you want it, but if it's placed improperly or at a slightly wrong angle, it can make it so that your knife, especially a larger, defensive knife, is going to print in a huge way. It's going to stick out. People are going to say, "Wow, that's a huge knife. That's sticking four inches deep into his pocket," or if it's sticking out very far, it's going to be obvious. Clip design has a major effect on concealment. There are a number of different after market clips that you can get for deep pocket carry. You have to consider that that's going to cost extra, over and above the cost of the knife and you have to make sure that it fits your knife. Clip carry is a great option, but it can be done very wrong also. The simple way to make sure it works for you is to try it out.

Dan: If you read a good review, it should discuss clip options. I happened to be left-handed, so when I review a knife it's very important to recognize whether or not it has options for people who don't want to carry the knife on their right side. That's important not only for people who are left-handed like me, but also people who are right-handed but want to carry their knife on their weak side. Maybe they have a firearm on their right side and they don't want to carry their knife on their right side. It's critical.

Rob: Another characteristic of the knives that we haven't covered is the locking mechanism, and there are a number of different locking mechanisms. They all have their advantages and disadvantages. The most common lock is probably the liner lock, but there are many others. In my opinion, the biggest decider is whether or not you are able to open the knife or close it with one hand. Most of these are strong enough for everyday carry use. What's your opinion on that matter?

Dan: I agree. The way that a knife opens and locks in place is very important. As you said, there are dozens of locks available on the market currently. There are several considerations. Are they ambidextrous? How easy are they to engage and disengage? Can you do it with one hand? As far as deployment goes, you have your thumb-studs, your thumb-holes, assisted opening knives, flippers, the Emerson wave, etc. You have a bunch of different things to look at that are going to very important on a knife you will be reaching for multiple times, every single day.

Rob: Going back to the locks, I don't want to overemphasize here. Different models will have greater strength in how they're able to hold the blade, but for the most part, they are going to be safe. They don't want to sell a product that will give them lots of liability and get sued into the ground. There are some designs that are weaker then others or not well executed, but you can read reviews and find out about those. The biggest consideration, in my opinion, is how you're going to close the blade again. It's different with a liner-lock versus a frame-lock or a lock-back. When you look at that, bear in mind that when you close a knife, you are not in a race. You never should be.

It shouldn't matter that you can close it with one hand, you should always be doing it carefully and closing a knife with two hands is normally not a big deal. Getting it out quickly in a defensive situation is important. Deployment speed is important, but after the fact, when you're done using it, you don't need to be in a hurry to put it away. Just keep that in mind when you're looking at the lock. Don't put too much emphasis on being able to close it quickly and with one hand.

Dan: It's probably less of an issue than being able to deploy it easily, but there are some knives that can be opened and closed easily with one hand and I might see that as a slight advantage over one that can be opened easily, but not as easily closed. It's definitely a factor. Not a deal breaker for me either, so I totally agree.

Rob: One other thing that I consider when I'm looking at a knife is the assembly hardware. I don't want to see something that's riveted together. Some people will never take apart their knife. They'll never clean it. They don't care. It will be different for different people. You may not care about this at all, but when I'm selecting a knife, I want something that has screw heads that I have the tools for. I want them to be something that's relatively common. I want to be able to take it apart for cleaning or modification.

Dan: That's very important because typically, these knives will need to be cleaned and adjusted, especially if something happens like submerging your knife in salt water or getting a bunch of mud in there. Maybe you need to lubricate the hinge or if it's an assisted-opening knife, you may have to apply some extra lubricant or grease to the inner workings of the assisted opening mechanism. It's important and that's a sign of a high-quality knife. Typically, the lower quality knives are completely riveted together. There are exceptions to that rule, but yes, you want to look for that, because that's important. If you're serious about knives, you're going to want to invest in a little set of torque bits. You can pick up a set at your local hardware store for under 10 bucks, and that's what most of these knives use. Most don't use conventional flathead or Philips screws. You also want to take a look at overall fit and finish.

Rob: Fit and finish is such a difficult thing to judge in a review. It's very much comparative, and if you don't have a reference it's difficult to really judge this. When someone's looking at fit and finish, the main thing is they want something that's not going to fall apart, that's going to keep working for them. What are some of the best judges of fit and finish?

Dan: You want to examine the knife closely. You want to see if all the pieces line up. For example, if the handle has multiple pieces, you don't want a lot of gaps. You don't want a lot of loose parts. If you look at any metal surfaces, you want to see that everything's been polished and is smooth and rounded. You don't want rough corners or screws that are sticking out through the knife at odd angles. You're looking for overall reliability for the just general quality of it. It's somewhat conjunctive. It's definitely comparative, but you can tell the difference after you've handled a number of knives both poorly made one and well made.

Rob: This is not a make or break. If you get something that has a few gaps, it's probably not going to fall apart on you. It doesn't mean you've got the worst knife in the world. As long as it meets your standards you're good, but it is something to consider.

Dan: Especially in the context of price. Price is kind of the great kind of balancer of all this stuff. You've got to take all these different parts, all these different facets, and then say, "This is a $20 knife so we'll give it a pass", or "This is a $200 knife and this is totally unacceptable."

Rob: You could spend $5,000 and expect to have exactly what you want in every single aspect of what we've talked about, including perfect fit and finish, but not everybody's got $5,000. Find what aspects are most important for you. Where are you able to settle concerning fit and finish? What blade are you willing to work with that's already set up in a production configuration with the other aspects that you want? There are enough knives on the market that you're going to find something that will work for you.

I know a lot of people that get all worked up over a certain brand. By "worked up" I guess you'd say they're loyal. They only buy a certain brand. Do you have any certain brands that you think are a cut above the rest that you'd recommend people to check out first?

Dan: I try to take an objective view on this. I really have to because I'm operating a service or a website where I'm reviewing knives. I certainly don't want to show particular allegiance to one company, but brands are so powerful, especially with today's world of marketing. They communicate important signals about quality and about past values. There are certainly a lot of trusted brands, but that doesn't mean that a particular brand can't make a knife that doesn't work for you. Even if they don't typically make knives that you like, that doesn't mean that they can't make one that you do like. For people just looking to get into EDC knives, I would recommend Spyderco, Benchmade, Kershaw, Cold Steel, or Boker. Those are some of the bigger brands out there with production knives available at prices that pretty much anyone can afford.

Rob: That's a great list of places to start. Remember that production or quality control cannot catch every mistake. Some people may be dead loyal to Spyderco because they ended up with Kershaw knife that happened to slip through quality control, yet they always happened to get perfect Spyderco knives, or vice-a-versa. You never know. That's the way that it is with production knives. Every single knife is not individually examined in the way that a custom knife is. If you get a bad knife, you may want to try that brand again later. It could just be that specific model, or just quality control and it slipped through.

Dan: That's also a good opportunity to really get to understand the company by determining how far they'll go to stand behind their products. If you get a knife that you're not satisfied with from any of those brands that I've listed, you should be able to go to them and give them your complaint. They should be more than willing to fix the problem for you or replace the knife. If they're not willing to do that, that would breed some disloyalty to the brand. Certain people are just going to like a certain brand.

Rob: Maybe because they like the logo, right?

Dan: Because they like the logo, or they like one thing or the other. It's a free country. You can buy whatever you like. I do enjoy a variety of knives, and that's what makes collecting fun for me, the differences. It's fun examine those differences.

Rob: We talked about hardware, and the ability to disassemble and worked on the knife easily with simple tools. It's also important to find out whether or not parts are available for the knives. Unfortunately, this is not a very common thing, but if you're going to be working a knife hard or if you're going to be modifying it and you want to make sure that you have back-up parts, verify this in advance. Sometimes you can buy extra scales, extra handle pieces, extra lock parts, and that's just something that you might want to take into consideration.

Dan: And sometimes companies will give you a new pocket clip or a new screw if you happen to lose it.

Rob: Dan, I appreciate you coming on the show here and talking with us about this.

Dan: It's really been my pleasure, Rob. It's just great to be a part of this. Thanks again for having me.

Defensive Light Use and Selection

Dave Spaulding was awarded the 2010 Law Officer Trainer of the Year Award. He is a 30+ year Law Enforcement & Federal Security Contractor veteran. Dave was a founding member of his Agency's SWAT Team and performed hundreds of forced entries. He spent 12 years as its training officer. Dave spent five years as a full time use-of-force instructor, and another five years as the commander of a multi-jurisdictional drug task force working major narcotics cases from Seattle to Miami. He has worked in corrections, communications, patrol, evidence collection, investigations, undercover operations, training, and SWAT — and has authored more than 1,000 articles for various firearms and law enforcement periodicals. He's also the author of the best-selling books Defensive Living and Handgun Combatives.

Dave is also a graduate of most of the major shooting schools including Thunder Ranch, Gunsite, Mid-South Institute of Self-Defense Shooting, Smith & Wesson Academy, SIG-Arms Academy, Heckler & Koch International Training Division, Lethal Force Institute, Beretta Training Division, CQB Services, Ltd. and Defense Training International.

Rob: I want get your thoughts and your opinion on the importance of lights.

Dave: Keith Jones told you that he was a product of his yesterdays, and I like to say that I'm a product of my life experience. I worked a lot of years on patrol. I spent time in narcotics. We ran a drug task force and I spent a lot of time working nights and doing a lot of stuff like entry work and building searches. I've searched for my share of bad guys in the dark, and did pretty well with it. I never got shot, and we seemed to apprehend all the people we were looking for, but it just seems like, toward the end of my career and since I've retired, there seems to be a whole new wave of training in reduced light capabilities. I have been to some of these classes put on by the major manufacturers of lights and some private institutions, and I guess I just don't see where some of the tactics and techniques that are currently popular have jived with my personal experiences.

Some of the things that I've learned while I was strobing and darting and rolling and diving across doors and into rooms, in recent years were overly complicated compared to what I experienced in my police career.

Rob: I don't have any low light flashlight training, and I'm sure that it's very different, the flashlight training that a police officer receives versus what the average civilian on the street needs or wants. The average person that's walking down the street looking to protect themselves and their family, is not going to be chasing --if you are, you've got serious issues-- criminals through buildings, rooting people out, etc. I know we do have police officers listening/reading, but the average civilian is not going to be in need of those sort of tactics, right?

Dave: No. You need to understand that there are a lot of armed citizens out there. Responsible armed citizens. I'm not trying to demean them in any way, but there seems to be a certain trend among armed citizens and police officers alike to try to emulate the Special Forces community and the things they see with the Navy Seals, Green Berets, Delta Force, or even some of the combat contractors like Blackwater or Triple Canopy, yet much of the stuff that those special mission units do, doesn't translate well to what the armed citizen or the law enforcement officer is going to do. It's overly complex. It's reliant on special gear. That kind of stuff is just not going to come into play if you're trying to search your home in the middle of the night for an armed intruder, or even for a police officer that may be looking for a burglar.

Where I have differed with some of the better known reduced-light trainers and schools that are sponsored by the manufacturers is in how to use the light. I realized early on that the human eye worked a whole lot better in daylight or artificial light than it did in darkness or inconsistent light. Darkness is not the real threat. It's inconsistent light. I'll give you an example. You're walking behind a building or down an alley and there's a floodlight, a security light above the door to this business. Across from it is a dumpster and behind that dumpster is a dark shadow with dark pockets. You may be able to see a person standing over there, but you can't see what they got in their hand because the hand is in the shadow. Think about when you're walking across the parking lot at the shopping mall or out and about or walking through your neighborhood. It's not that it's dark. The problem is that the light is inconsistent.

Your eyes can adjust to darkness or they can adjust to light, but they really can't do either one well. We all realize they do light much better, so we have white light sources, or flashlights as they're commonly known, to help light up those dark pockets. I'm sure there's going to be some experts or authorities out there that are going to tell me I'm all wet, but you know what? For 30 years it worked real well for me: If I had to go into someplace dark, I'd flip on the lights!

"Wait a minute, Dave, you're giving up your advantage of being in the dark." What advantage do I have by being in the dark? I found out pretty early in my law enforcement career that eighty-plus percent of the time, if you could hook your arm around the door-frame and wave upward, you're probably going to hit the light switches in that particular room. When we'd be going through businesses, warehouses, or homes looking for burglars, robbers, or whatever the case may be, you could hook your arm around there, flip it up, and you would light up the rooms and your eyes could see really, really well. I wasn't trying to rely on this little tiny flashlight beam, which wasn't near as good as they are now.

We found that if we did have a suspect in a business or a locale of some sort, we could flip on the lights and actually chase him back where we wanted him to be, because they would seek the darkness. They felt more secure in the darkness because they were criminals. We would flip on the lights and basically we could chase them back into the room where we wanted them to be anyway so we could take them into custody. That type of thought is totally contrary to what is being taught now in many of the schools.

Rob: People may say that you lose the advantage, but you might say that it levels the playing field. Even initially, you have the control of when that light comes on and what you're ready for at that point.

Dave: "Dave, you're standing in the darkness and you have the ability to use that light in their face." That's all well and good if you know where they're standing, but how are you going to put the light in their face if you don't know where they're standing? By flipping on the lights in the room, I'm now in the dark because the darkness is behind me instead of the light being behind me *outlining me*. If I flip on the lights in that room, especially if it's a large area like a warehouse or a large office space, now I can use my eyes the way God intended them to be used: In the light! They're not designed to be used in the dark. We're not very good in the dark.

Rob: It's not even necessarily the darkness or the light, but the transitional period is where it's the worst. I remember when I was a kid my dad used to talk about the rods and the cones.

Dave: Absolutely, and everybody realizes it. This is not rocket science. You adjust to the darkness pretty slowly. It can take 20 to 40 minutes, depending on your age, whether you smoke, and a number of other factors, but your eyes adjust to the light pretty quick. You may blink a little bit, but you see in the light pretty fast. I would do everything I could to make it *bright* whenever I could. At traffic stops as cops, we have floodlights, takedown lights, and the light bar to light up the area, because we just work better in the light.

You've got to remember that that a flashlight, when you light it up, illuminates where you are located. The bad guy realizes that that flashlight has to be attached to a person in some way. If you were a bad guy hiding in the dark and somebody comes in and they start strobing, where do you think they're going to direct their fire if they decide to shoot at you?

Rob: Hmmmm... I wonder?

Dave: They say overwhelm them with the light, and they've got these lights that do all this strobing stuff. If you've ever been behind some of these lights, when they strobe they can almost overwhelm you. It's like being in a disco in the 1970s. This is another case where we're training for our rules, the good guys rules. We won't shoot at anything if we don't know what it is. The bad guy is going to see us coming in there with that dynamic $300 strobing light trying to strobe the room. All they're going to do is take their 15 round 9mm pistol, and light up the area, just shooting in all kinds of directions. I don't want to cast dispersions on these various training programs, but I think many of these things are more tacti-cool then practical in that they're overly complicated and too reliant on gizmos.

Rob: So in your opinion, the best tactic concerning low lights, or lighting in general, is to add as much light as possible because your eyes are going to adjust to that more quickly.

Dave: Yeah, light it up. That's the way your eyes work, and only use the flashlight when you truly need to.

Rob: Nowadays also, these flashlights can literally disorient and temporarily blind, even in the light.

Dave: This is not a new thing. We even knew back in the '70s when we had the Kell lights and the B-lights and the flashlights that were basically the size of a tailpipe, that if you flashed the light in someone's eyes that it would make them blink. It would make them turn their head. We also realized that it wasn't a very long process before they could orient themselves and they could respond to it. That whole thing about putting a light in their eyes is nothing new, but remember it's just a momentary technique. It's something to disorient them so you can do something else. The light in their eyes in itself is not going to overwhelm them to the point where they're going to quit.

Rob: Say someone is out on the street at night walking with their family back from dinner. The bad guy steps out of the shadows. He's in full light. This person has a light maybe right next to their magazines, and they have their gun. What are they going to be doing with the flashlight? They are threatened. In that situation they're not going to be going for the flashlight first.

Dave: If they're walking with their family and they're doing a late night stroll on a nice summer evening, I know in my particular case, and probably in that of most of the people I know, the flashlight is probably going to be in their off hand, and not so much because they're concerned about attack. They just want to be able to use the light for those times when they truly can't see. If it's dark, or if they hear a growl off to the side, they can use the light to see what's over in the dark spot.

If that person does pop out, they can bring that light up and they can flash it in their eyes, but now they've only got a couple seconds. They've got to come up with another plan, because I don't care how many lumens that light is, when you put it in their eye, they're not going to drop down grabbing their eye sockets, screaming in agony. They're going to turn their head! They're going to blink, but then they're going to do something. So you've got two, three, or five seconds to come up with some kind of a contingency plan. The light is allowing you to get ahead of their response.

You had better be prepared to take some sort of action. If nothing else, relocate yourself from where you were at the moment you put the light in their eye so that when they do come back looking for you, you're someplace else. Now you've added a little bit more reaction time to it, but be prepared to confront them, strike them, shoot them, or whatever may be appropriate or reasonable based on the circumstances at hand. The flashlight in itself is a disorientation tool. It's not really a weapon in the sense that it can incapacitate or disable.

Rob: When you're under duress or threatened, it is only a temporary tool, but when you have it out in advance, it can also aid your awareness and keep people away that realize you're aware and ready for them.

Dave: Exactly.

Rob: I don't claim to get in the mind of an irrational attacker, but if it were me hiding in the shadows, I would say that the person who is keeping an eye out where they're walking and using a flashlight is not exactly the best target.

Dave: The flashlight that's in your hand is like the gun that's in your hand. It's prepared to be used. It's ready. You are prepared to act with that implement. If it's in your pocket or in your pouch or whatever the case may be, now you have to access it, or basically draw it, just like you would your firearm. The great thing, though, about a flashlight versus a firearm is that having a flashlight in your hand amongst society at large is not alarming. People don't think nothing of it. "He's got a flashlight in his hand, so what?"

Rob: It's socially acceptable.

Dave: You can keep a flashlight in your hand most any time and nobody is going to get worked up about it. If they did say "Hey, what's that in your hand?" "It's a flashlight. I just bought this thing, I think it's kind of neat." Nobody would think anything of it. If you needed it, pow! You hit that tail cap, you pop them in the eyes with it, and then you change position, prepare to act, or get ahead of their response loop and do various things, but again, you have to have it in your hand. You have to have preprogrammed what you're going to do if this happens. Then, we get all back to that whole thing about mindset again.

Somehow we always come back to mindset, don't we?

Rob: Yes we do, and awareness. When we were talking with Keith, he was talking about the attackers' triad, and one of the legs of their triad was stealth.

Dave: Right.

Rob: You can take that stealth away from them by using the flashlight where you might not even need to. Maybe you're walking along at night and you just kind of flash the shadows. You have it out and you're using it. Maybe you're pointing it at the ground in front of you. Not flashing people in the face as you walk by, but just using it, showing that it's there. It takes away that attacker's stealth. He realizes that he's not going to be able to get close without giving himself away.

Dave: Every attacker has some kind of a plan in his head. It may not be anything very formal. It may be very informal. It may not even be very structured, but he's got something in his head that he is going to do, and anything you can do to disrupt that plan, to interrupt his thought processes, basically intercede his ability to act, is going to give you an advantage. If you can do something that he does not expect, you're going to be better prepared to respond to a threat. It's all about doing the unexpected.

Rob: We've talked a little bit about overall general doctrine in the use of lighting. I personally think it's best used as something that will keep attackers away, at least in the hands of civilians. We know that we want as much light as possible. That makes it easier. I'm sure a lot of people want to know your opinions or your thoughts on firearm-mounted lights?

Dave: They are a supplement to a handheld light. I know in the law enforcement community, and with some of the armed citizens there's that desire to have the light on your gun. It is a great tool in the fact that it allows you to keep both of your hands on the pistol or revolver(there are some revolvers with rail systems on them now). It allows you to keep both of your hands on the gun to shoot. However, you've got to remember that any place you point that weapon-mounted light, you are also pointing the muzzle of that gun, and you don't point the muzzle at anything you're not willing to shoot, kill, or destroy.

That being the case, the handheld light can be pointed in directions that the weapon-mounted light cannot be. So the weapon-mounted light, to me, is the same as it was when we put them on shotguns, submachine guns, and now carbines. Is it is a supplement to a handheld light. You can do so much more with a handheld light. There are things you can do with the handheld light that you can't do with the weapon-mounted light. However, the weapon-mounted light has the advantage that it allows you to place both of your hands on the gun. You can shoot with the handheld light, but I don't care which of the various positions you're using, you're still shooting with one hand, because the support hand is going to be occupied by the flashlight in some fashion.

Rob: I have found that lights mounted on guns, by the way, do cover far more area then just the area that the muzzle covers. I don't know if I'd necessarily want to use that to search for something...

Dave: You can splash, but you still got to point the muzzle in that direction, even with the splash of the light. If you're going down your hallway and you catch something out of the corner of your eye with that light, what do you think you're going to do with it?

Rob: Jerk it over that way.

Dave: You're going to point it in that direction, and it may be your kid with a glass of water in their hand or it may be a burglar. So the idea behind the handheld light is that you can divide and conquer.

Rob: Is it worth having to get special holsters and having to deal with having the flashlight on the firearm just for the limited situations where it's very useful?

Dave: I think a weapon-mounted light on a home protection pistol is probably a great idea. For the handgun that you've got in the dresser drawer next to your bed, or whatever the case may be. You may be opening doors or pushing family members out of the way and need the free hand. Let's face it, in conflict, are there going to be times that you're going to be willing to point the muzzle of your gun out into the unknown to illuminate it? Yeah, let's be realistic. If we look at the rules of gun safety you should never do that, but in armed conflict there may be times when you're willing to point that pistol and that light at things that you don't know 100% whether it's a threat or not.

I don't want to say never, but I think as a general rule, the handheld light gives you more options versus the weapon-mounted light. But again, I'll be the first to tell you that the weapon-mounted light, especially on long guns, is a good supplement to a handheld light.

Rob: When you visualize these situations, you think in advance what it might be like, what you might be doing. There are so many situations, and you almost have to make it an odds game. What is most likely to happen? What situation am I most likely to encounter? Will this be a hindrance or will it be a help? Is it worth the extra complication or not? There are a number of questions that each of you have to consider for yourself. It depends on where you live, where you'd be using that light, or a whole slew of different deciders. You have to figure out whether or not it's going to be worth it to you. You think not a concealed gun, but you would want it on a home defense handgun, rifle, or shotgun? Something where you think it would be a great supplement to a regular handheld light?

Dave: Sure. On a weapon where it would probably stay in place all the time. A police officer's service pistol, a home protection gun, a SWAT handgun. Those kinds of things. It's probably not a good idea to be taking it on and off because you don't know when you're going to need it. Put it on a gun where it's probably going to stay. Like you said, war game the situations. You're thinking ahead, which is great. What are my likelihoods for this particular weapon? What do I intend to use it for? If it's one of those situations where the light is probably going to stay on the gun all of the time, then it's probably a good accessory. If it's a situation where the thing's going to be coming off and on, then it's probably not a good accessory. The handheld light would be better mate for that particular weapon.

Rob: I know this doesn't necessarily relate to flashlights, but if you have not had the opportunity, make sure you go out and shoot in a low light situation. Make sure it's a controlled situation, but you really should at least see what it's like. See what your sights look like in that sort of situation. Make sure that the lighting system that you have, and its intensity on different colors, is not going to wash out or make your sighting system more difficult. If it's something that you think you will have in your home for at night, make sure that you set it up accordingly. It doesn't have to be night or day, but make sure that it's something that will work in that night situation with ultra-bright white or yellow lights on the target. The way you find that out is by going out and trying it.

Dave: Right, and I would caution our readers, don't just go to your gun club's indoor range, flip off the lights, put a target down there, and shoot. That's not reality. You need to go someplace where maybe you could throw a road flare over here, and you've got a light back behind you, and maybe a set of headlights from your car are pointed in that direction, because that's reality. It's not that it's consistently light or consistently dark, it's the inconsistency of the light that will cause you the greatest problem because you cannot adjust to both. Your eyes will see better where it's light, and you'll use the white light in those pockets where it's dark. That's where the white light comes in. That's where it's essential.

Rob: So do we even want to quote the cliché statistics about how many gun fights happen at night or in low light situations?

Dave: Three out of four.

Rob: Unbelievable.

Dave: Yeah. That is if you're looking at the law enforcement statistics. Understand that these are taken from the law enforcement officers killed statistics. That means the officer lost. In those statistics, three out of four happened in low or inconsistent light, and at least 45% of the time there's more than one suspect involved. I don't think that it would be too much of a stretch for the armed citizen who is facing criminal attack, because let's be honest. Criminals are plying their trade at a time when they think they can best get away with it. Darkness makes them less liable to get caught, so that's when they're going to be out. They're going to feel more comfortable in the dark.

The armed citizen or the law enforcement officer has to prepare themselves so that they don't feel uncomfortable in the dark. That takes some adjustment both in mind and in personal preparation, but it can be done. I don't fear the dark too much. I spent a lot of my police career on night shifts so that doesn't bother me too much anymore. By the same token, I keep my tactics, I keep my tools for reduced or inconsistent light applications pretty simple.

Rob: What you mentioned about multiple attackers is another case for having multiple lights available.

Dave: Yep, because you could be engaging this person and looking the light in another direction. I don't know who first said it, but I know Clint Smith from Thunder Ranch popularized it when he said that one is none and two is one. What he's talking about is the ability for a tool to fail you when you most need it. Having two of something, is a good idea. It's like a police officer that has a service pistol but he has a back-up gun. Well, he may have a weapon-mounted light but he also has a handheld light. Having two of something that is considered critical equipment is probably a good idea. If one fails, and of course Murphy is alive and well and he does have a sense of humor, you'll have something to fall back on during a critical incident.

Rob: Even barring failure, just thinking of the fact that if you have one that is keeping someone else under control or keeping them at bay or illuminating something, and there's someone else running around, you're not going to want to leave the person you are holding in the dark, give them free rein, basically, and go and find this other person. So that light is out of commission essentially.

Dave: I hope I never find myself in a situation where I'm holding a person at bay with my weapon-mounted light and using my handheld light in my off hand, trying to search in a different direction.

Rob: That's where you should be running?

Dave: Think about what's being required of you to divide your attention that way. Can't say it won't happen, but boy, talk about a nightmare scenario. That's probably it.

Rob: Is there anything else we need to cover here, talking about low light and talking about flashlights?

Dave: It's like anything else. We're not going to hit too much on equipment because equipment doesn't win the fight, but having good equipment is worth it. Have a good flashlight, have one that you can rely on. I'm not too much for flashlights where the tail caps do multiple things. Momentary on or off with the press switch, twist the tail cap for constant on. Two different functions for two different things. It's pretty simple, straight forward.

I don't like the things where I've got to push in and turn one thing to get to do this, turn two positions to get it to do that. You're not going to do that under stress. So get yourself a good light that's simple to use. Get a lot of lumens. How many lumens do you need? I think if you've 70-plus lumens you're probably good. Is 100 or 200 better? Maybe, but by the same token you've got to remember, if you've got a 200 lumen light and you go into a bedroom that's maybe 20 by 20 and it's got white walls, can that 200 lumens overwhelm you? You bet. Keep in mind what you're trying to accomplish.

I tend to keep a pretty compact light that's got 100 lumens or so. It's an LED so if I drop it, it's not going to pop a bulb. I've done that several times with the old xenon bulbs. I can remember one time I was trying to work my way up into a crawl space looking for a narcotics suspect. I can't remember if I smacked the light on the edge of something, but I dropped it. It hit the floor below me and it popped the bulb, so now I didn't have a light. Any element of surprise I may have had in this endeavor was gone. I like having the LEDs because they're pretty rough and tumble. They take a lot of abuse, and now they're so bright with these Cree LEDs. I keep them pretty simple. I try to keep them bright, easy to use, easy to carry. Simple is good.

Rob: I don't know if this is something that everyone does, but I'm a cheapo guy and I have a hard time replacing batteries when they may not be out all the way, but I finally forced myself to. I marked on the calendar so that every two months I remember to change out all the batteries in all my red dot sights and in my weapon-mounted and defensive use flashlights, to make sure that they're topped off and ready to go. It doesn't have to be two months. For some people you may say, "Wow, that's way too long." Some people may set it for three months. Whatever it is, make sure that you're at least checking them and making sure you have batteries that are going to work.

Dave: Sure, and especially on long guns, it's very easy to keep a spare set of batteries on the gun, in the grip of the AR, or whatever the case may be. For the handgun, you keep a spare set of batteries where you store your handgun with a weapon-light. I have a light mounted on the wall in my truck, so I have a spare set of batteries in the truck there. I think the important thing is that you don't just ignore it, that you monitor the life of your battery. With these lithium batteries, they're a bit expensive but they've got a shelf life of like 10 years. Now we have lithium AA batteries and batteries are just better than they've ever been. I hear all this stuff, you don't want to trust batteries, but that's bunk.

Rob: Trust, but verify.

Dave: The pacemaker that's in our grandfather's chest is run off a battery. The car that we go out and get into every morning, whether it's hot or cold, runs on a battery. You can depend on batteries. You just want to be prepared for their failure and their replacement, but to say don't trust anything with batteries. You have to. We do it every day, all day long, all the time.

Rob: If you have kids also, don't let your kids play around with those flashlights either and run down the batteries.

Dave: No, no. Give them the little cheapie flashlight that's got Elmo or something on it. Let them run around with that. Don't let them fool around with your serious equipment. I know they're going to want to, but don't let them.

Rob: Yeah. I remember as a kid I'd always take my dad's military gear and try to play with that. You know the old angle-head flashlights, the military ones?

Dave: Yeah, right.

Rob: We used to take those, change out all the colored filters, and when my dad would get ready to go out for military drills and he'd have to dig around and find those things, and figure out if they were working, where the different covers were, etc. Keep them out of the hands of your kids, as much as they'll want to play with them.

Dave: Sure. Just don't bring the flashlight to their attention. Just put them away and don't let them see you with them, and then they won't get curious. This is lifesaving equipment. It's not something to let them fool around with.

Rob: You can keep your kids away from the guns. You can do the same thing with a flashlight that's meant to be used in nearly the same capacity.

Dave: Absolutely, and if they do by some chance see you with your flashlight, or whatever the case may be, just be prepared to give them a little cheapie inexpensive flashlight. They're not going to know any difference. They just know that daddy had something pretty cool and they want to play with it. Well, here. Hand them one. They'll be happy. This is from personal experience with having three kids.

Rob: I talked to a holster maker several weeks ago and he said that somebody, a major name in our industry/sector, had a holster set made. It was a matching set for flashlight, mags, and the gun also, but he also had one made in the exact same color, exact same style, everything, for his kid. It was to hit a little toy gun so that he could have the same set-up that his daddy had.

Dave: That sounds like a pretty good dad. He was thinking ahead, and he took care of the little guy. Yeah, that's a pretty good solution.

Rob: Well, I guess that's a little off the subject, but I think that we covered most of what we wanted to. Can you think of anything else that we left out here?

Dave: No. Really we've just kind of got started in it. Some of your listeners out there may disagree with me, because all of this reduced light and owning the night training is all in vogue right now. They may disagree. They may think that some of the fancier techniques are the way to go, and that's certainly their choice. I'm talking on the basis of my experience of looking for honest-to-God real bad guys in the dark. Keep it simple. Use your eyes the way they're intended. If you can make it light, make it light, and use the flashlight only when you have to. I think those simple rules will go a long way.

Rob: Like you said, this is not the only way. It's just what you've learned from your experiences. I read not too long ago where someone was talking about fine motor skills, or things that are more complicated and how some instructors will dismiss them because the majority of people are not going to be able to handle these things under stress. The majority of people may not be able to, but there are some people that will be able to handle it. There are people that will be able to practice and practice and practice to the point where they can handle something that's more complicated. We aren't saying that these more sophisticated techniques, won't work for you, but for the majority of people they're not the best. Find what works for you. Dave, thanks again for taking the time. I really appreciate it.

Flashlight Technology and it's Progression

David Chow is a flashlight enthusiast turned manufacturer. He is the founder of 4Sevens, an innovative company that focuses on bringing performance LED lights to market at affordable prices. His knowledge and passion is obvious in the interview below.

Rob: We're here to talk about everyday carry flashlights. David, why don't you tell us what makes you qualified to speak on this subject? Tell us a little bit about your background and what you do for a living.

David: Well, I started a flashlight company about six years ago, just at the eve of the LED revolution, when the LEDs started producing serious amounts of light, enough to potentially can replace the incandescents. I call these power LEDs because they're driven at a higher current, producing a lot more light then traditionally what LEDs can put out.

Rob: You talk about this LED revolution. I remember not too many years ago, when everyone had incandescent flashlights. I remember these huge, two C-cell batteries were the norm. I'd take those things to camp, and you could hit people over the head with them, and they didn't put out half of what you can get with a small little AAA light nowadays. How long ago would you say that this revolution started? I know it's not something that happened on a certain day, but where did the major breakthrough innovation happen? About what year?

David: I'd say 2003-2004 when LumiLEDs came out with their Luxeons. That's when the LEDs started to grow up.

Rob: So that's still relatively recent!

David: Yes, within the last decade.

Rob: So you got started about that time. When did you start making lights?

David: I started modifying lights for people about '04-'05. It was kind of a hobby, and eventually turned into a business.

Rob: So how did it turn into a business? Did you just have enough work that you said, "I see demand here, I'm going to go full time?" How did you make that jump?

David: At that time I was actually working full-time. So it was mainly an evening thing to bring a little bit more to the table. I was modifying flashlights for people. At some point it got a little overwhelming to do custom work, and I met some guys in Asia. Today they're known as Phoenix. They started by selling LEDs to street vendors. We hit it off and talked about product. By the end of '05 we were cranking out some pretty high end flashlights, which was unprecedented up to that point. These were lights that used aircraft grade aluminum alloy and housed high-powered LEDs. The very first light was driven by a single AA, the most common battery on the planet, and most available. To be able to put out 30, 40 lumens from a single AA was just simply unheard of at that time.

Rob: So now were you just working with their product that they had, or did you start collaborating right away? How did that work?

David: Well, they were actually on Candlepower Forums. They kind of showed up and showed some ideas. CPF was quite a smaller group and less uptight then they are today, less commercial. People shared ideas in a fairly open forum. A lot of ideas were tossed out. I saw some talent in these guys, hooked up with them, and they actually did have a light that was like stainless steel, something kind of crazy, and we talked product. Eventually, we came together and produced a light that people still use today.

Rob: Now, let's talk about everyday carry back before the LED revolution. I remember people still had mag lights that they had in their pouches, and people still carried keychain lights, but obviously these things were not putting out nearly the power that they are now. How has this LED revolution changed people's everyday carry habits? Do you see a lot more people that are actually carrying lights, or do you just see the same people that are carrying better and brighter lights? How do you think that's affected people?

David: There are two factors concerning LEDs and everyday carry. Technology-wise, the ability to carry something very bright on your keychain is now a possibility. So many people are beginning to carry lights on their keychain, simply to wow their coworkers, friends, and family. It's such a night and day difference that they say, "I've got to have one." Compared to the old solitaire mag light, which they actually still sell, it's a complete night and day difference.

The second factor I'd attribute it to would be the whole concept of fire back in prehistoric times. To have fire allowed you to control your environment, what's around you. Without it, you were vulnerable. When the sun sets, you don't know what's around you. Light, actually fire back then, allowed you to control your environment. I think the whole Zippo phenomenon gave people the sense of power or control over their environment, stemming from prehistoric times, I'd say.

Rob: For everybody's lifestyle, this is totally different. For some people, it gives them so much more freedom or so much more power over the darkness. I understand this here in Nepal, where right now we have power outages of eight hours a day.

David: Wow.

Rob: Those are just the scheduled rolling blackouts. When we first moved here, we had no power inverter. We had nothing to run back-up power. I remember there were certain times of the day where the lights go out. Yes, you have lanterns. Yes, you have flashlights, but it severely limits what you're able to do. When you have the lighting, it just opens things up. Not only does it change your entire attitude, but it changes what you're able to do.

David: And the ability with LEDs to put out light at low levels, is also a huge factor. For our brand, 4Sevens, we have a unique feature in some of our lights. It's called a moon-light mode and with any ordinary battery you can have up to 30 days of continuous run time. Actually, in independent tests we've had nearly 60 days, and with just a common AA. If you use it at that level for two hours continuous everyday, that one set of batteries will last you an entire year! You can't do that with incandescents because you're heating up a metal wire.

Rob: No, there's so much wasted energy there. So we've got these technological marvels, we've got these tiny flashlights, we've got all this neat stuff. Getting more efficient emitters means several things. Number one, you can put out a lot more power with the same size batteries or number two, you can shrink it down and put out the same amount of light in a much smaller package. I know you guys have taken this in both directions. I'm sure you see a lot of people that are purchasing and making purchasing decisions and reaching out to you all. What kind of decision making process do people make when they're deciding which route to go, with something that they're going to try and have with them every day?

David: There are different kinds of everyday types of uses, and first I would identify your application. If you're just a casual user, you might want just a light to have on your keychain. If you're an officer needing a duty light that you'll be using at least an hour everyday, that's a different kind of need. You might some need kind of a rechargeable set-up. Another kind of EDC type would be for emergency situations, where you keep the light on you, but you don't use it everyday. You want it available, ready to go for emergency situations. All those come into play when you have to decide.

I would start from battery type. Typically, alkalines are just terrible for emergency situations. Number one, they spontaneously just leak for whatever reason. To have a light that either is depleted or doesn't work because it's leaking is worse than a rock because you can toss a rock, but a flashlight sticks with you until you have to put new batteries in.

A lot of people don't consider this. The lithium battery technology is well worth looking into, because number one, they typically have a 5-10 year life span versus 1-2 years with alkalines(if you're lucky and if it hasn't leaked yet). Number two, the lithiums have higher power density, which means they are lighter. You carry less and you get more power from the battery. Alkalines also stop working when it gets close to zero degrees, but with lithiums they'll work well below zero and in high temps as well.

A year after I got married, I took my wife to Yosemite and we camped out and hiked. That night, it snowed. It was like six or eight inches, and we got lost. Completely lost! Well, I whipped out my GPS. It had been leaving the tracks from the day before, and I was like, "No problem, we'll get back." It turned out I had a bunch of alkalines. They did us no good. I kept alternating batteries from a set under my armpit(keeping them warm) and switching them around with the GPS so that it would operate for just a few minutes before it would shut down again.

Having lithiums is can be critical. There is a reason why the government, when they use flashlights, uses lithium CR123As. The power's available, it's reliable, and it works in extreme situations. If you're someone who needs a light, but maybe you don't use it every day, it just needs to stay there and not destroy itself. Lithium definitely is something to consider.

Rob: Lithium is for a light that you're not using on a regular basis but you want to know that it's going to be ready when you need it.

David: Yeah.

Rob: If you're using it on a regular basis, you see when it's running down. You see when it locks into a low mode and you know you have to replace the battery, but something that sits in your glove compartment, or something that hangs on your keychain and gets used rarely, you want to make sure that you're using a lithium battery because it's going to store energy better and not leak as much.

David: I know people balk at the cost of the lithium cells, but I believe they more then pay for themselves. I've had lights that when I needed them, at the very critical moment in time, say you have a flat tire, it's not there for you.

Rob: Are there any particular brands of batteries that you prefer above others?

David: I would say stay away from kind of no-name brands. I would stick with Duracell, Energizer. We actually spent a considerable amount of time sourcing a good lithium cell that, number one, performs on par with the best cells available, and secondly it's properly sourced with the safety mechanisms and quality control.

Rob: We talked about use cases and how it affects the battery that you choose, if you're going to be using it often versus going into storage for an emergency light. Use case is the first thing that you're going to come up against, but a lot of people that don't have a flashlight are somewhat unaware of exactly how they're going to be using it. They may move to other deciding factors.

Some of the biggest things that people are looking at are price, the amount of light that they're getting, and the size of the flashlight. Depending on your priority, you're going to look at those first and use them to narrow down your choices. Let's talk about the lumens, the performance. First of all, tell us a little bit about comparing lumens. Is it apples to apples across different brands, or how do people look at this?

David: Five years ago, everything was compared using watts(power consumption). That was the de facto standard. One watt LED, three watt LED, seven watt LED, but I'm happy to be part of the force that changed that. We were actively educating our customers that wattage doesn't tell you anything. That just tells you the energy consumption, and actually some of our one watt LEDs are brighter then some of the three watt LEDS, and it's brighter than 7 watt incandescents .

Rob: Because they're much more efficient, right?

David: Correct. So as the LED revolution progressed, every year and a half we'd see close to double the efficiency. It's kind of like cars giving you about 10 miles per gallon. Every year and a half it becomes 20, 40, 80 miles to a gallon. That kind of a jump that is a huge factor. So when you just talk about wattage, it doesn't tell you anything. Then there are so many ways to measure light. There's candle power, foot candles, lux, but why do we choose lumens?

Lumens tells you the total amount of output, total amount of light that comes out from the LED. It doesn't take into account the reflector, how cumulative it is, the surface brightness. That's lux, which has to do with distance and all this kind of stuff. Lumens just tells you how much light is coming out. It's kind of like horsepower to the car, not top speed.

Rob: When you compare it to horsepower, that would be horsepower measured at the flywheel as opposed to at the rear tires, because we're not talking about with the reflectors in the actual light.

David: Right. That's another kind of measurement. The LED manufacturers, Cree, Nichia, they all give you a rating. That rating is at the LED and it's actually theoretical. They measure it in the labs, but under certain temperature, humidity, special conditions, and for the early LEDs, they would give you specs based on impossible conditions like having it in liquid nitrogen to keep it cool.

Rob: Not very helpful!

David: So a lot of manufacturers would quote and base their output on LED specifications, and it wouldn't be wrong. They are the specs that the manufacturers gave you, but the actual amount of light coming out, there are some losses. For example, just glass will take up to easily 10% off the top. If you have like coated lens, it could drop down 1% or 2%, it depends. If you touch it, your fingerprints will absorb some light. The reflector affects it, and the optics. Anywhere the light has to bounce or move around, there are some losses, and this is natural. Just like a car, there's horsepower at the crankshaft and then horsepower at the wheels. Even past the wheels, the actual result of propelling the car depends on if the wheels slip, this and that.

Rob: The performance, yeah.

David: There are so many things that could reduce the original amount of lumens, sSo what we've done is we've started a new rating. We call it out the front(OTF), meaning we measure the light output out the front, and that's the number we give people. Unfortunately, everyone's still playing the one-up game until it's ridiculous. We're calling 1,000 lumen lights, a million candle power. It's just ridiculous.

Rob: Everyone knows, higher numbers are better.

David: Rrrrright.

Rob: That's a brave move on your part, taking that step to reality, because it's going to be a lower number than someone else who decides to throw out their statistic given by the LED manufacturer.

David: Yeah.

Rob: It's definitely a more practical measurement. Now, let's talk about reality as far as what's actually coming out of the light.

Can you give us an idea of what do these lumens do for you? How many lumens do you need to see while you're taking a walk vs. trying to blind someone? What are some of the practical realities of what certain amounts of lumens can actually do for you?

David: The human eye is really amazing. It has a very dynamic range of sensitivity, unlike anything out there. We can adapt to full, all out sunlight or we can be in pitch black and just the tiniest amount of light is enough for us to navigate. So it varies. It depends on your situation. The moonlight mode in our 4Sevens lights is called moonlight, literally because the spot intensity is about the same as on a full moon night. You can literally navigate with that kind of light level, and that is about 0.5 lumens. With a reflector, it throws enough light that it's usable.

Age also comes into the equation. Older people probably need more light because of their eyes, and definitely the more the better. I would say 50 to 100 lumens is probably what's needed for most applications. If you need more reach where you need to throw light further, say in a tactical situation, 200, 300, 1,000 lumens, whatever you can get will help.

Rob: There are advantages to having a very small amount of lumens. People will look at some of these things and say when am I actually going to use the low setting? Personally, I carry a Preon 1, and the low setting quoted out the front is 1.8 lumens. It's a small light, but that low setting is what gets used, literally, 99% of the time.

Only rarely do I have to ramp up and use something the second or third level on this light. Even with that lowest setting, if I'm using that at night in bed beside my wife, trying to read, I'm very glad that it's not anything brighter because it would be disturbing. There are a number of factors that can come into play that make you grateful for these small, low settings.

David: That's part of what's unique about LEDs. Eventually people will start citing run times instead of lumens. We started in '09 to create lights that have an incredible amount of run time. Imagine, say cars that will give you 200 miles a gallon. If you're not in a hurry, they'll get you from Point A to Point B. It may be slowly, but it gets the job done.

And when you need it, you step on it. With our Preon 1s, we have it come on on the low setting, because you're right. Most of the time, it does the job. Why waste energy? Why contribute to battery waste? If you look at the number of batteries being recycled or tossed away every year, it's phenomenal. I don't have the stats in front of me, but imagine one battery for your light in a year vs. a bucket full of batteries. With incandescents you don't have a choice other than the maximum.

Rob: Let's talk about the high end lights. We talked about the advantages of having the low-end lumen output. Let's talk about the reality of the difference between, 1.8 lumens and 70 lumens, or even 200 and 300 lumens. What kind of perceivable differences are we looking at when we compare, say, maybe 300 lumens to 400 lumens, or 400 to 500?

David: Well, the human eye detects things logarithmically, and pretty much all our senses are on a logarithmic scale, except for tactile pain. If you punch me twice as hard I'll feel twice the pain. As far as our other senses, it's logarithmic. This means you need three or four times as many lumens before you'll see twice the amount of light. So with the difference between 100 lumens and 200 lumens, you'll notice the brightness, but you won't say, "That's twice as bright !" You need about 300 or 400 lumens compared to 100 lumens to say that it's twice as bright.

You've got to consider the impact on the battery life. It decreases fourfold for a two-fold increase in perceived light. So 100 lumens vs. 200 lumens you have a twofold difference in run time, but for the actual application, maybe you don't need 200 lumens. Maybe 100 lumens will do.

Rob: So the reality is the lumen wars are only nice if you've got to make sure you have a brighter flashlight then your buddy.

David: Yes.

Rob: But in the real world, you're better off --unless you're going to be tripling, quadrupling your lumens-- just sticking with that light that you have, rather then upgrading just for another 50 lumens.

David: That's right, but lumen wars are still valid from a manufacturer's point of view. All the car manufacturers are touting their horsepower, but if it's 10% more horsepower, you're not going to feel it. If you have instruments, you can measure it.

Rob: On the other end of the spectrum. Moving down in lumens. When you've been using a light that's at a certain level and you step down, it is noticeable and almost bothersome too.

David: But if you're hiking, and you're using medium mode, and you say, "I don't want to walk back in the dark." Which is better? Run out halfway back on the trail using high mode, or dialing the brightness down, knowing that you'll have enough light to make it back, and more?

Rob: It's nice having those options and those settings. We have talked a little bit about the lumens. Now let's talk about size. You have lights that vary in size from your Preon Revo, which is just a miniscule little thing, essentially a keychain light, on up to some monstrous lights. I saw a prototype spotlight that you guys have. Unbelievable stuff! So for size, where do you start with this? Where do most people begin? Do they start out big and then shrink down to what they want, or do they start small and then move up when they realize they need more lumens? How does this work for most people?

David: Most people start out with the smaller lights, mainly because of price. They are more accessible and easier to pick up. Then again, it just depends on your needs. The bigger lights, the higher output, higher end lights tend to be more specialized, and people have to justify the cost. That big monster light you saw was actually developed because of a military inquiry. They wanted an LED light that can just light up a whole field, and we developed it for them. Probably less than 0.001% of people will actually need 18,000 lumens in a handheld application.

Rob: "Need" is a very interesting word when it comes to lights. So you've got quite a range to choose from. You've got to choose from your lumen range, you've got to choose from your price range. Now, let's talk quickly about the interfaces. The most common interface among your lights is probably the twisting head interface, right? What is most common?

David: Well, as far as what we sell, the twisting one sells by far the most, probably because of the price point. The twisting head is simpler, but I would say a lot of people prefer the tail switch because you get direct feedback from it. Whenever you add a switching mechanism, it does add to the size and length to the light, which in turn affects your EDC-ability, the ability to carry something small and light. Maybe it's only a couple of ounces, but a couple of ounces on your person multiplied by however many hours you're walking around, multiplied whole year, adds up. Bulk is not nice on your keychain either, unless you really like a huge keychain.

Rob: Yeah, I know some people with that.

David: It's efficiency with mass.

Rob: The clicky tail-cap switch is definitely nice for tactical or high-end lights.

David: Yes. Tactical lights typically need a little switch in the back. They need to be able to activate, deactivate instantly. Actually, the word tactical is pretty over-used these days.

Rob: No doubt. People name anything tactical if they color it black. As far as people that are using them with weapons or in combat situations, it is nice to have a clicky tail cap, but that's also nice for just about anyone. Are there really any situations where you would prefer the twisting head interface versus the clicky tail cap?

David: It's preferred for compactness, particularly as the light gets smaller, every little increase percentage-wise makes a huge difference. The twisty is also very quiet, if that's a factor.

Rob: No, that's absolutely a consideration.

David: There's also some extra reliability as well, because with the switches, it's a latching mechanism that could get stuck or fouled up. The twist type is very intuitive. The disadvantage is that you pretty much need two hands. It's not a one-handed type of operation. For a duty light, you probably would want a switch, but for something on your keychain, a twist type light is just fine.

Rob: David, I appreciate you taking the time here to talk with me about this and go through some of the different specifications, some of the different characteristics of these lights for everyday carry.

Flashlight Features and Recommendations

Marshall Hoots is a flashlight enthusiast as well as the owner of GoingGear, an online retailer that sells over 400 different types of flashlights. He regularly helps customers with flashlight selection and offers some great insight.

Rob: Why don't you start out just by telling us a little bit about your background with flashlights.

Marshall: I've been kind of fascinated with flashlights for most of my life. When I was a little kid, my dad used to make fun of me because we'd go on day hikes where there was absolutely no possibility that it would ever be dark at any point and I'd have six or seven flashlights with me. This all started at an early age with me. I've always been pretty fascinated with them. I worked in the corporate world for a pretty long time during and after college, but I got tired of it and wanted to start my own business. I started out selling survival items like fire steels and paracord and eventually I got to the point where I started selling flashlights. That's when everything pretty much exploded.

Rob: As a business owner, I'm sure you encounter a lot of demand. You see what people are using, what people are wanting. You see some of their decision making processes. I'm sure you deal with a lot of people, even one-on-one. Can you tell us a little bit about what the market looks like for EDC flashlights nowadays? What are people moving towards, or gravitating toward?

Marshall: We sell quite a few different flashlights. We're up to, I think, 500 different models at this point. We see pretty much the entire range of the market. We get your backpackers, we get military, we get police, we get just regular people, we get enthusiasts, and people buying as gifts. We see people carrying pretty much everything. As far as an EDC flashlight, the average person usually tries to go for something smaller, one or two cells, that they can slip in their pocket, or at least in a smaller holster, and then when you start talking about your military and police guys, that's when you start talking about the bigger flashlights that they'll carry on a regular basis. They'll start carrying the ones that are weapon mountable, have a strobe with quick access, etc. Except for the huge ones, pretty much every flashlight we sell can be found in a holster on someone's belt.

Rob: For EDC gear, it starts out differently for everyone, depending on what their use case is going to be. When people start looking, they look at the lumens, they look at the brightness of the light. They want to have the super awesome bright light, but normally that's not what you're going to end up carrying. Tell me, when you started out with flashlights, and I know technology has changed a ton just in the last few years with what is possible and what's available, but how did you start out in this? What were you looking for when you were searching for your first flashlight, and then how did it change as you found out more about what you could carry?

Marshall: When I first started out, I was a little kid. You had the crappy plastic two celled incandescent kind of lights, and that was all that was available 20 years ago. I'm 31 now, so when you talk about when I was five or six, that was pretty much all that was on the market. You had your big 4 D cell mag lights that everybody knows about. That's what a lot of military and police were using. That's what a lot of them still use. Then you had companies like Surefire come out. I wasn't even aware of them until relatively recently. They started coming out with the concept of a high end flashlight. They broached the idea that a flashlight could cost 60 bucks or 100 bucks, and you could get the quality that was worthy of costing 60 bucks or 100 bucks.

I think it was when China got into the game, specifically Fenix, that things really changed up for everybody. The first one that really got me interested in the more modern flashlight market is the Fennix L01. It was just a little single mode Fenix light, powered by a AA battery. I think it was actually their first model. I got it six or seven years ago, and the thing put out, I believe, 60 lumens, and that was just amazing at the time. When you're talking about a 4 D-cell mag light putting out 20 or 30 lumens with four D batteries, and a single AA LED putting out 60 lumens, it was revolutionary. It's just kind of grown leaps and bounds since then.

Rob: Let's talk about making the choice and choosing your flashlight. We're not going to be able to make the choice for every person that's listening to this show, but we can at least point them in the right general direction. The majority of our listeners are not necessarily flashlight enthusiasts. They're not the ones that are out there looking for the perfect interface. They just want something that's going to meet their needs on a daily basis. It will help them look underneath the bed. If the lights go out, it will help them get to a bigger flashlight or the inverter system, or the back-up generator. What sort of flashlights are going to meet their needs?

Marshall: It depends on the specific person, and this is a question we receive so often that we actually went and purchased some new software for our site that can specifically help somebody trying to find the perfect flashlight for them. You can filter the lights by the manufacturer, the color, all that kind of stuff. We have about 20 or 30 different things that you can filter with. If somebody is looking for a single cell AA flashlight from Fenix that has a cool tint, you can go and find it quickly and easily.

That's how we help people find flashlights, but for a general kind of purpose, we try to focus in on a few different things that people are looking for. One of the biggest deciders is going to be battery type. That's usually where we start, because some batteries are a lot easier to get than others, and some have more benefits. For instance, AA batteries, everybody knows them and probably has a hundred of them sitting around, but they don't necessarily offer a whole lot of power for their size. With an enthusiast or somebody working in a harsher environment you start talking about CR-123, the lithium batteries, because they have a lot wider temperature operating range. They'll have a lot longer shelf life. You can get up to 10 year shelf life on them, and they offer a lot of advantages. Unfortunately even on the cheapest, decent quality lithium batteries, you're still talking about $1 a cell, and some people aren't really willing to pay for that. Batteries are usually where we start.

Rob: You mentioned a wider range of temperature operation. Is it that they don't perform at their optimum outside of that range, or is it that they drain a lot faster? What are the negatives or the downsides of having something that's not set up to be used in your temperature, your climate?

Marshall: It's actually both of the things that you mentioned. Alkalines don't have a very wide temperature operating range, especially when it starts getting down into the lower temperatures. I'm not sure what the actual temperature is, but at the colder, below freezing temperatures, they'll actually stop working. The internal chemistry doesn't work with them. The CR-123s and other lithium batteries will work and work well in a much wider temperature range. That's why a lot of the military and law enforcement people doing things that are in a little bit more of an extreme environment tend to prefer those kind of batteries.

Rob: Or even people that are going to stash that in a car that's not kept in a warm garage. That thing's going to get pretty cold at night and pretty hot during the day. During the summertime you're going to have a wide temperature range. You don't want that thing just draining on its own while you leave it there.

Marshall: For people that are stashing them in their car, lithium batteries are definitely more popular, and they do make lithium AA batteries. Energizer makes some lithium AA batteries. You don't get quite the power performance that you get with the CR-123s, because you're at three volts with the CR-123 and about 1.6 volts with the Energizer lithiums vs. a regular alkaline's 1.5 volts. With the CR123 battery you can get a higher voltage, which can mean a higher output in your flashlight.

Rob: You were talking about your software and I'm looking at it here on your website. It really is great. It reminds me of Newegg.com. I'm seeing that you can break it down by manufacturer, color(for those of you style aficionados), LED tint, max lumens, min lumens, number of modes, strobe, whether or not you've got the SOS beacon, whether it includes a holster, or the type of LED. I'm just going down the list here. You've got some great stuff. You've got a ton of different batteries, and most importantly for a lot of people, you can even break it down by price. So it's a great tool for starting out.

Let's go down through some of the other deciding factors that people are looking at when they're looking for their flashlight. I know we don't want to hit all of these or it'll take us all day here, but after the batteries, what are most people looking at?

Marshall: Usually we try to get people to focus in on size. If you're talking about keeping something in your pocket all day long, that's going to help us narrow it down. We're going to eliminate all the larger lights and all the more tactically oriented lights, because they're not as comfortable to carry in your pocket.

If you are comfortable carrying a larger light, you can get a lot more out of them. You'll be able to get more throw, which means the beam will go further. You'll get more distance out of it, and generally speaking, the larger the light, the more you can get out of it. You get more features.

Rob: If you want a very small and very bright light, you're going to pay a huge amount of money, or you can get a very bright light at an average or larger size that will be a lot cheaper. You have to weigh the factors in there and see what size you can handle. Where would you recommend that most people start if they've never carried a flashlight before? Maybe they've carried a pocket knife or something in their pockets before and they figure, "That's where I'm going to carry this." Where do you recommend that they start? Do you recommend that they start with a CR-123 light that's just the same width all the way down, or do you think they should start with a AAA or AA? Where do you recommend they start?

Marshall: I usually try to steer people towards the CR-123s, but these are people that come into the store. They may be a little bit more of an enthusiast. For the average person, I would say definitely stick with your AAs or your AAAs, just because they're so easy to find, and you can still get really solid output with them. With two AAs, you can get 200 or 300 lumens very easily, which is as much light as most people need. Of course, as soon as they see that 600 lumen light or that 1000 lumen light, then that's what they want, but the average person sees 200 lumens and they're completely blown away. The average person is probably better off with AAs just because of how easy they are to find and how inexpensive they are.

Rob: So tell me, just to satisfy my curiosity, how many people do you know that are carrying 1000 lumen lights with them as EDC flashlights?

Marshall: I'm sure there are a few enthusiasts out there, but most of the people that have told us they've done this are military and law enforcement. they've already got a belt full of stuff anyway, so having another thing in a holster isn't really that big of a deal to them.

Rob: We're talking about size. You can get a lot of power out of a two AA batteries. That's where you'd recommend that people start, and that is where I started also. I agree. Then from there, you can say, "This is too much light for me. I've used it so little, all I need is a AAA" and step on down to something, or you can say, "Hey, I'll move up into the enthusiast realm and pick up something a little more powerful, or something that will allow me to get more light." So after the size, what would you say is next? The interface or the light that it puts out?

Marshall: I would say interface, and include in the interface the kind of modes that it has. You will see this on a lot of the enthusiast sites like candlepower forums or EDC forums. People will talk about strobe and SOS and beacon and all those flashing modes and how they wish that companies wouldn't include them. I always make sure to tell manufacturers that that is the absolute worst thing that they could do if they want to keep on selling lights, because after max output, strobe is the number two thing that people ask us for, especially when you're talking about law enforcement. Bouncers or guys in security use strobe on a daily basis. It's a very important tool to them.

That's one of the next things that we ask. "Are you looking for any special modes? Do you want it to be able to strobe? Do you want any kind of programmability or anything like that?" We'll get the response and go from there. Usually the only thing people are asking or wondering about is the strobe.

Rob: A smartly set up interface will allow you to change it and adapt it to what you want and will leave some of these functions that are not so often used out of the front end of the interface.

Marshall: A nice innovation that we've seen a lot of companies do in the last year or so is use two switches instead of just one. You can actually use the two different switches to quickly switch between your different modes. One of our companies that we just started dealing with about a year ago is Klarus, and a lot of their lights are ones with the dual switches. You can instantly access max output or you can instantly access strobe, and you can quickly switch to your other modes that you need. That has been a really nice innovation that they've come out with. The rotary ring is a ring that turns up by the head that'll let you quickly access your different modes in a little bit different way. I's also a really nice innovation that they've been doing in recent years.

Rob: There are some creative interfaces out there, but it's really up to you. The first flashlight you get has a large influence on what interface you're going to be comfortable with down the road. So a lot of people that are just starting out, they're not going to be thinking, "I must have this interface". They're going to try out something, see if it works for them. Is there an interface that you see that new people prefer? What's the simplest, or most convenient right off?

Marshall: There have been a few companies that have been kind of bucking the trend in making simpler flashlights, like Klarus and Jetbeam. They both have lights in all the regular battery configurations where all they have is two modes. So when you have the head tightened on the flashlight, it's your max output. You loosen the head and you have a lower output. That's it. There's no strobe. There's no SOS, nothing fancy. Those are the lights that I always point people towards if they're buying them as gifts. If they're not sure what kind of enthusiast the person is or if they're not the most technologically inclined person, then having a light with only two modes is super simple and very easy to figure out. The nice thing is, it's even better if they never figure out that they can loosen the head. It's even simpler for them. They think it's just that one mode light, and they're good to go.

Rob: This is the age old debate between simplicity and more features. You can choose whichever you want, but just know what route you're going when it comes to the interface.

Marshall: And that's something that we try to help people clear up with all the YouTube videos that we have. People can see the interface, how they actually work, how they perform outside, because I know a lot of these flashlights can be daunting. When you're talking about spending on some of our more popular flashlights $250$300, you want to know upfront what the interface is and how it's going to perform. We try to help people figure all that out before they actually plunk down $100, $50, or even $20 on a flashlight.

Rob: What about the types of actual switches? Heads turning versus clicky tail caps?

Marshall: That's definitely another preference. One of the big advantages of having the twisty head where you loosen and tighten it to operate the flashlight, is that it takes up almost no space. If you want the most compact flashlight possible, one you can just throw in your pocket and forget about or have it on your keychain, then a twisty is a really good way to go. I personally don't like them at all. I don't like using the head of the light to operate it. Not that it's bad to use one handed, because most of them are able to be used one-handed. I just prefer a press switch. It's definitely a personal preference, whether you prefer the switch on the side, the switch on the end, no switch at all, or two switches. That's another thing we like to do with the videos, show people how they operate so they can get a better idea of how they would be using it themselves.

Rob: When you talk about the size of the switch, it really depends on the size of the flashlight. When you put that on a double CR-123 flashlight, it's not a huge difference.

Marshall: Right.

Rob: That's part of why it is so much more prevalent in those flashlights, but when you stick that interface, the clicky tail cap, on the end of a AAA light, most of the time it adds a good 20% or more to the light.

Marshall: That is why very few manufacturers that are producing in large quantities make AAA lights with tail switches on them.

Rob: And it's difficult to engineer when they get that small.

Marshall: That's another problem that they have. A lot of times you'll see them with simpler interfaces just because the size of the circuit they have in there, to make it cost effective. You can't have a lot of the advanced features on the tiny lights.

Rob: So you trade off on the interface with the small lights. The biggest disadvantage of a twisty head, is that you're going to be using two hands. Sure, if you practice enough and you have the dexterity, you may be able to use one hand, but if you want to get it out and use it quickly, you're going to be using two hands. That's the biggest disadvantage. You just have to see if your lifestyle and the way you're going to be using this flashlight is intense enough that you have to have that clicky tail cap. It could just be a matter of comfort or personal preference, but you're going to have to make that decision.

Marshall: Definitely.

Rob: Past the interface, past the size, past the batteries, have we finally come to the lumens yet?

Marshall: I honestly try to avoid that discussion, even though it's usually the first thing that people ask for. When I'm helping somebody find a flashlight, I try to steer them away from thinking about lumens, because honestly, they're not a very good measure of what you're actually going to be getting in the light. Lumens are a measure of all of the light that's coming out of the front of that light and depends on where it's measured.

The new ANSI standard is what most people are going toward. I'm not exactly positive what it is, but I believe it's after three minutes from a foot away or something like that. It doesn't tell how big the hotspot is(that bright part in the center). It doesn't tell any kind of throw or distance that you're going to get. It doesn't tell how big the spill is, how big the angle of the beam is, or anything like that. I usually try to steer people away from thinking about that, and try to get them to watch the videos or get the lights in their hands so they can actually turn it on, and see how it really performs, because you never really know until you've turned that light on.

Rob: When it comes to the actual lumens, are there certain minimums for different tasks?

Marshall: It really depends on who you ask. A few years ago, if you talked to Surefire, they said that the minimum that you would want to have in a tactical situation, which basically meant the minimum amount to blind somebody in a darkened area, was something like 50 lumens or 75 lumens. Now, most of their lights start at around 200 lumens. You keep on seeing things go higher and higher. You can get away with higher numbers and saying that you need higher numbers, but it really depends on what the person is going to be using it for.

Another thing that you'll see in some of the newer, larger LEDs, is that people are going to turn them on and they're going to think the lights aren't as bright. They have three times the lumens, but the lumens are much more spread out over the beam and it's not going to look as bright. For minimum lumens, I'd say if you get at least 100 it's definitely going to be a usable light. In a compact light like a two AA 200 lumen light, you'll be able to go out to about 100 yards, which is pretty awesome for a light that size.

Rob: You've got to think about the fact that people survived on these lesser lights forever. So what is necessary? It's a very qualified question. Even when you put the qualifications on what you had heard from Surefire, you were talking about a darkened situation. A dark situation is different for every person. Are we talking about dusk, or are we talking about dead of night, are we talking about with moonlight out? What is necessary is going to be very different for every person. I was just wondering if there were any rules of thumb as far as what most people are looking for when they're looking for a tactical flashlight, or something that they'd use to temporarily stun somebody versus somebody that's looking for a EDC flashlight just to light the sidewalk in front of them as they walk in a dark parking lot. You're saying there is nothing specific. You just have to check it out.

Marshall: Exactly. Until you actually see the beam, it's going to be kind of hard to say what's actually going to be good for you. The really nice thing about most flashlights these days is that almost every flashlight we sell has multiple modes. So if it maxes out at 500 lumens, that doesn't necessarily mean you need to use it at the 500 lumens. So you can drop it down to one of the lower outputs when you don't need that max output, and you get a lot better battery life. You can get your 6 or 10 hours at 100 lumens, or if you need to bump it up, you can bump it up to that 500 lumens for the situations where you do need that max output.

Rob: Let's get back to hotspot and spill. I'll give you a really dumb example of how this has become important for me. When I first started out with flashlights, other then the old-fashioned incandescent monster lights, I just thought these things were the coolest ever. Hey, as much light as I can in as small of a form factor as possible, the better. Sure, the interface is nice, and I was just coming onto these different features, but I got to where I was using these tiny flashlights at night to read my Kindle. This is situation I don't want to spill a ton of light over onto my wife sitting next to me there and keep her up. You want something that fits this situation. I found that I was gravitating toward a certain flashlight because I could hold it in a certain spot that was comfortable, and it would spill over the entire Kindle but not go too far. Every person is going to have different needs. This is not something you think of right away, but it is something that is important, and it will vary according to what you're using your light for.

Marshall: I'm completely in agreement with that, because I ran into the same situation. I was reading my Kindle in the bed, and I had a flashlight that had a very defined hot spot(the bright part in the center) and then the spill around it, which is the dimmer light, wasn't even remotely as bright. So I had this really bright defined hot spot, and it would only light up a small area of the Kindle the way that I was holding it, and you get this kind of tunnel vision effect. It's not very good on your eyes, it's not the most comfortable way to read.

Rob: And you find yourself shifting the flashlight a lot.

Marshall: Exactly. So I switched over to a flashlight that basically did not have a hot spot, it was just pure flood. The entire beam was basically the same uniform output, and it was a lot easier to read. That's definitely a consideration as well.

Rob: Where else does this come into play?

Marshall: I think the biggest time is when you're doing up close work. Some of the really popular backpacking headlamps like your Petzel Tikka and your Princetontech will have just a small, little five millimeter LED with no reflectors of any kind, because most of the stuff you're doing when you're backpacking is close up kind of stuff. You're looking around in your tent. You're looking in your backpack. You're reading a book. You don't want that tunnel vision, so you don't want that hotspot. I think that those lights are great for anybody doing any kind of outdoor stuff where they don't need that distance. There are a lot of lights, or a lot of headlamps, that will let you switch between.

So they'll let you choose a distance kind of beam or you can flip up a reflector or put on a diffuser for more up close work. Those lights are even better, but you also have the option of getting a more diffused beam headlamp for your up close stuff, because that's generally what you're going to be using the headlamp for, and then carry a flashlight as well for the distance stuff.

Rob: The distance stuff is always fun. I know there are the tactical applications, but I always love going up on the roof and spotlighting cows and they wander by. As far as an EDC flashlight that someone is going to carry everyday, are most people looking for a combination with a medium hot spot and a decent flood, so that when they're doing close-up work it's not going to blind them or be too differential? What are most people looking for?

Marshall: Exactly what you just said. That's usually what people are looking for, a mix of everything. A general purpose setup where you can do up close stuff. Maybe it's not the best for reading, but it'll do an okay job and still have some distance to it where you can light up things 50, 60, or 70 yards away.

Rob: You see people that talk about the newest and the latest LED type. Is it really something that people are really concerned about, or can we just look at the other stats, the other features, and not worry about the LED itself?

Marshall: It is kind of important and depends on what you are using the light for. The new Cree XML LED is a much larger LED than what people were generally using in flashlights before. If you're using a larger LED in the same size light with the same size reflector, you're going to get a much more floody beam. It's going to be more spread out and it's not going to be as good for distance. You definitely want to look at the LED in it's case, because if you get the smaller LED, even though it's going to have a much lower lumen output, you're going to get better throw. If distance is important to you, then you would want to go with the smaller LED with the lower lumen output. It's kind of counter-intuitive.

Rob: So it's the combination of the size of the LED with the reflector. You see what it's thrown into, and you'll have to extrapolate it from there.

Marshall: That's why we try to have videos for almost every flashlight we sell. We try to have videos for all the lights just so people can see what kind of beam it has. I think that's a really good way to compare it. You can actually look at two different videos. I always use the same conditions and see how the beams compare to each other, because the same light with two different LEDs is going to be very different in terms of performance.

Rob: Tell us about the LED tint and how important is that to most people?

Marshall: The average person honestly doesn't really care. I'm one of those people. I do not care at all. I don't care if it's green, I don't care if it's blue. That stuff really doesn't bother me at all. For some people, it absolutely drives them crazy. Both thoughts are completely valid. It's just what's important to you. There are three more popular tints these days. Cool white is what everybody is used to seeing with your LED lights. It's that pure white light with a little bit of bluish tint to it. That's what most people are thinking of when they think of an LED flashlight.

There's also neutral which is a little bit on the warmer side. The nice thing about Neutral is that it gives a better color rendering. Your greens and your browns look more green and brown. Some people don't like the color. I find it to be kind of nice, but I don't really care either way. One of the newer tints that they've come out with is called "High CRI." It has really good color rendering. It's something like 90% of what you would get with sunlight. That tint has been pretty popular lately. They give you really nice color rendering, but it only matters if that's important to you. Some people see it and they see it as orange or a reddish tint and it drives some people crazy. It's definitely worth taking a look at some pictures online, or taking a look at some videos and seeing, if that bothers you or not. Do you like it one way or the other?

Rob: So you could almost compare it to sunlight, a normal yellowish incandescent light in some cases, or even a CFL, the white light. If that sort of stuff annoys you or bothers you, check out the tints. Otherwise, don't worry about it.

Marshall: If it doesn't bother you, go with cool light because they have the highest output. That's what the vast majority of our customers do. They get the different tints by putting a coating on the LED. The more of the coating that they put on there, the less light can get through it.

Rob: So there's a little bit of a performance tradeoff with any of that stuff that gives you the better color rendering?

Marshall: Definitely. High CRIs have something like 30% or 35% lower output compared to their cool light counterparts.

Rob: Marshall, I appreciate you discussing this with us. I think we've covered a lot of good information and given people some reference for them to make their decision when they choose an EDC flashlight. Make sure you go and check out goinggear.com. I really do like that software you've got for narrowing it down. It makes it easy to see what your options are when it comes to the things that you care about.

Marshall: Thanks for having me.

Preparing for Medical Emergencies

Michael "Doc" Hewitt is an 11 year veteran of the United States Navy. He spent 5 years as a Security Specialist, specializing in Patrol, Communications, Special Investigations, and was a member of the Special Response Team. He then transitioned to become a Corpsman (Fleet Marine Force) and was assigned to a Marine Corps Force Reconnaissance Company. During his time with the unit he participated in or was an instructor for numerous Special Operations training packages, all while being responsible for the health and safety of the Reconnaissance Team both at home station and while deployed.

Leaving the Navy in 2001, he began working in the Middle East and Europe as a private security contractor, as a member of a Personnel Security Detail and as a Force Protection Specialist.

Upon returning to the United States he went to work at the Federal Air Marshal Training Center in Atlantic City, NJ, teaching advanced pistol marksmanship, concealed carry techniques, and tactics to Federal Law Enforcement Officers. The Federal Air Marshals are known as having the most demanding and rigorous firearms training programs in the country. While there, "Doc" had to exceed their standard in order to become an Instructor and then took personnel with varied levels of skill and taught them to the demanding standards of the Federal Air Marshals.

"Doc" recently attended the Department of State's PSD program as well as the DoS Firearms Instructor course, and was sent to the Middle East to train personnel for the largest Embassy in the world, the United States Iraq Embassy in Baghdad. He has been a full time, professional firearms instructor since 2004 with no accidents, injuries or mishaps.

Greg "Cruz" Grutter *is an 18 year veteran of the United States Military, with 7 years in the Marine Corps as a Scout Sniper and Lead Scout Sniper Instructor for the 2nd Marine Division, having participated in Operation Just Cause. "Cruz" then did 6 years as Police Officer and Corrections Officer, with time as a SWAT Instructor and Team Leader/Commo/Breacher. Working approximately 11 years as a Federal Air Marshal under 3 different administrations, FAA, TSA, and ICE, he was an Instructor for his Hub as well as Instructor for the FAMTC. He created policies and procedures in support of the firearms program and established TTP's for the Defensive Tactics (Unarmed) program as well as helped establish TTP's for several Allied Air Marshal programs.*

Working for Governmental Intelligence Agencies for over 2 years, "Cruz" stood up the first security detachment in support of covert and overt intelligence gathering operations. He conducted training for all government agencies and military personnel in country as well as foreign nationals in support of OEF. Was team leader of the protective service detail on over 1000 missions in two years protecting flag rank military officers, high-ranking diplomats, and U.S. and Foreign Government Officials.

Rob: Despite your military backgrounds, I want to talk with you about medical preparation for civilians. We may end up coming around to the military stuff, or at least referencing it, but most of the readers live in a civilian setting and they don't have the same needs medically as the military does. Unfortunately, many people think this means that they don't have to worry about medical issues with their everyday carry. That's not the truth, is it?

Doc: No, definitely not. When you can bleed out from an arterial wound in four minutes and the average response time in most major cities can be anywhere from 10 to 20 minutes, I would definitely recommend some sort of medical training, first of all. Having a nice kit is not enough. It's the same way with a weapon. It's one thing to have a nice weapon, but if you don't know how to use it, it's just a bunch of metal parts. Your medical kit is the same way. I definitely agree that you need something for medical emergencies. You should always have something handy, or have the knowledge to make do with other things. There are a lot of things around that you can use for medical gear but you have to know how to apply it.

Rob: Let's talk about training first. That's the most important thing, because it doesn't matter if you have the best medical kit in the world or the best gear in your hands, if you don't know how to use it. It does you no good, and you've been carrying it around or you've had it stashed somewhere, wasting space, wasting effort, and essentially wasting your money. Where can most civilians go for some simple training? They don't want to go into the details. They don't want to go to med school, but they want to learn how they can handle some of the major issues that they may have a problem with. They want to cover the odds for themselves. Where do they start?

Cruz: First, do a quick assessment of the area that you live in, work in, or travel through. If you're living in a desert environment it doesn't do you a whole lot of good to get training in high mountain areas. If you're in an area where you're prone to accidents where you might have more of a bleeding situation. You need to get training that supports the area that you're in. I like to tell my students, "I'm going to teach you to fight in the arena that you work in." When it comes to medical, we need to do the same thing.

If I lived by the shore, I would have different things in my kit to support what I need to do. There is enough training available out there to be able to get some information on the class that you're taking. Find out what a basic level class is. Find out what an advanced level is. What do you really need to concentrate on now to save your life.

Doc: You need to think of your medical training as just another tool in your toolbox. Cruz is saying is that you need to get the right tool. If you're living in the mountains of Colorado, you need to be aware of altitude sickness and its signs and symptoms. I live in Tampa, Florida. Altitude sickness is not high on my list of things to worry about. I have different things to worry about here. You need to tailor your tool to your environment.

Rob: And to your lifestyle. It also depends on the things that you do. For myself here in Nepal, I drive around in a two-wheeler all the time. I don't have a car, so an accident in my situation is going to be very different then an accident in the US. If I was to have something happen on the roadway, my needs would probably be very different. We also have different types of illnesses here that I should prepare for and check the symptoms. That's why you should check with the person that you're training with and try to train in an area similar to where you might have these medical issues needs.

Cruz: When you live abroad, there's a lot of medical stuff that's available that may not available to us here in the United States, even antibiotics over the counter. If you go south of the border, you can get all kinds of antibiotics. You wouldn't have to see the doctor for your normal colds. Here, we can't get stuff like that. What do you have access to on an everyday basis that you might want to think about? These are the things that I want to have on hand before something bad happens.

Doc: You also need to have a little bit of knowledge about what you're doing. I was recently in Jordan and we had some guys that were working for us that were going to a local doctor, and for a scratchy throat they were taking Keflex, a powerful antibiotic. It ended up causing them a lot more problems than the scratchy throat and it took me a good 15 to 20 minutes to find out this guy had almost overdosed on Keflex because he had a scratchy throat. A little bit of knowledge can be a bad thing sometimes. You need to be aware of what you're getting and what you're taking.

Rob: Well, we see it overseas, but it's not just overseas. There are a lot of doctors in the US that don't know what they're doing a lot of the time also.

Doc: Yes.

Rob: So training really goes a long way toward understanding what your doctor is trying to do for you and how he's trying to help you. Medical knowledge and medical training goes a long way in a lot of different areas.

Doc: There are a lot of good sources for training now, starting with Boy Scout classes. There is a lot of good basic first aid taught in Boy Scout classes, Red Cross classes, or your Explorer programs. It's not so much that it's hard to find a class. A lot of the problem I see is that when something happens, you don't have time to really think about it. You need to react! Taking one class is usually not enough, and taking a class that just involves sitting in a classroom environment is not enough. You actually need to try and apply the simple stuff. We have done classes in the past where we've had students apply a tourniquet to themselves. They simulated a gunshot wound and applied the tourniquet to their right arm. That's a very difficult task if you've never done it.

Rob: We're talking about training here, and I'm looking on the Red Cross site right now. If you're looking for a place to go, I'd start here. There's a tab at the top, it says "Take A Class". You can enter your zip code and they'll refer you to classes that are in your area. That's a great place to start, but a lot of the time Red Cross is not going to cover a lot of the combat aspects, and a lot of our listeners are carrying firearms. The firearm is something that they have with them, and when you do that, you want to have the extra training to deal with firearm-related medical issues. Can you make any references or refer us to any places where you can get training specific to firearm related incidents?

Doc: There's a lot out there. You're getting into some advanced medical stuff and it's kind of hard. You get into liability issues, but there are still some companies out there doing it. We've played around with it with some of our law enforcement students and you're really getting into a liability issue, but the training is available. You may have to look for it and there's usually some vetting involved, but it is available if that's what you want.

I know that for a lot of companies, ours included, the liability issues get in the way of what we would like to teach. With my background, I believe that knowledge is power. I'd love to give you the knowledge, but unfortunately the medical community doesn't look at it that way. They look at it as if we're teaching people to practice medicine, but it is out there and you definitely want to get some exposure to some of those advanced classes if at all possible.

Cruz: In the politically correct world that we are forced to live in nowadays, if I was to seek firearms medical training, I wouldn't use the word "gunshot" at all. I would see if they had some type of puncture wound training that I could get, or impact wound training. I would try to make the mechanism of injury anything but the gun. In the end, it's going to be the same. A puncture wound from a handgun bullet is the same if it's from a piece of steel in a mill shop. I'd be careful to word it that way. It opens up a lot more doors.

If you stayed specific and you wanted to get some type of combat casualty care, there's plenty out there. You can do a Google search and find enough companies. Unfortunately, It's very restrictive on how much we can show. I know that on my deployments overseas in hot climates, everybody needed to learn how to do an IV. If I came back to the States and put an IV in somebody, I'm assaulting them by stabbing them with a needle. It's a touchy situation, but the wording and verbiage that you use to get those people to help you will also open up doors.

Doc: The medical community has put a big hold on a lot of stuff. If you look at what goes into EMT types, basic and intermediate paramedic, they're very restricted. So a basic EMT you would think could do quite a bit, but in most states they can't administer anything other then charcoal, and that's ridiculous. I could have a diabetic in front of me that's on the verge of dying, but I can't squirt some glucose into his mouth or put a piece of chocolate under his tongue to help him pull out of it. The laws state that I can't administer anything other than activated charcoal. It's a touchy situation, but like we say, the training is available if you talk to the right people. A lot of times, over dinner after class, you can pose some questions and get the right answers.

Rob: A lot of these classes are directed at medical or military personnel that are going to be overseas in a combat zone. It sounds like there's a lot of extraneous stuff that a lot of civilians might not want to go through. Are there any alternatives to this, or do you say, "Hey, it's not a big deal. It's not much extra. Go ahead and be a military wanna-be for a weekend?" What's your advice when it comes to that?

Doc: Cruz and I probably see it about the same. Training is training. You never know the situation. When correcting a firearm stance, do you know if you're going to fire one round or are you going to fire six? Make your stance as much as possible to handle whatever gets thrown at you. The medical aspect of it is the same way. You don't know what's going to happen. You don't know the situation you might get into. You can't just say, "Just go do a couple of Red Cross classes and you should be good to go." In today's day and age, you don't know everyone's situation or what they might get into.

A lot of this stuff can apply directly to a moving vehicle wreck as well as some sort of gunshot trauma or combat trauma. The rules apply across the board. If you can find it and you have access to it, I would go as far as possible. I recently attended a T-CCC class(Tactical Combat Casualty Care) again under the Department of State, and I found it excellent and actually learned a couple of things. Some stuff has changed over the years, as it always does, but a lot of it was just a really good refresher to make sure that some of that knowledge I gained back in the day is still valid.

Rob: So if you've got the time, the money, the wherewithal, more training is better. That's the rule?

Doc: Yes. I would not tell anyone not to seek it. You never know. It might apply to your two year old who has something crazy happen in the house. Next thing you know your two year old has a puncture wound, and just for lack of a little bit of training, you might not have the wherewithal to handle it. Training is always key.

Rob: Cruz, I really liked what you were saying about not referring to it as a gunshot wound. If you're looking at a class and trying to figure out what to take, make sure you reference the types of wound without referring to the defensive tools that you may carry. You want to make sure that your training does match up with those tools because accidents do happen.

Cruz: There are probably a number of like-minded people that are reading this now and talking afterwards. Three or four of those people can get together, call an instructor, and say, "Hey, we really like what you have, but we'd like to tailor it to this. I have five people that are interested in learning this skill set as opposed to maybe the three that you have listed. We'd like those two, and then could we add this one?" I don't see you being turned away.

If the students are telling the instructor, "We'd like to pay you to do this," it's a pretty good motivator. If you have a good legitimate instructor who's got a good depth of knowledge, they shouldn't have a hard time working with you on that.

Rob: You can also check your local community college for medical courses or instructors. They normally offer basic EMT classes, and I'm sure you can at least find an instructor and work something out that way also.

Doc: The basic EMT class is actually very good and would give you a good base of knowledge. In the military now there are a whole lot of EMTs compared to when I was in. There's probably an EMT in just about every squad. Not only are they going through the T-CCC courses that the military puts on, but they're also sending them out to the EMT courses in the civilian world. It's usually a two to three week class, but they get time in the ER, they work with the fire department, they actually might see and work on some injuries. I can't recommend the basic EMT class enough. If that's what you have available, that's a really good place to start.

Rob: I'm sure our listeners will agree with us by this point that training is very important and necessary if you're going to handle your kit properly. It's necessary even in setting up your kit properly, but unfortunately, the majority of our listeners are not going to go out there and get training. It may be because of schedule conflicts, finances, or time. I don't know what the issues are, but the odds are that the majority of them are not going to.

Doc: Sure.

Rob: Let's help these people. If you're not going to take the time to go get training, obviously you don't need to have all the equipment that you're not trained and there are going to be a lot of things that you're not going to be able to take care of, but what sort of things can you learn just by your own personal study, or basically with no formal training?

Doc: Get a basic CPR class. That's probably what you're going to run into before anything else, and then carry a one-way mask. They're easy and they're small now. If you carry nothing else I would probably recommend that and a pair of gloves.

Cruz: If the individual has got the life that we all have with a wife, children, and community commitments, ant they just don't have the time for these things, get on a website or a blog or in a talk group, and run some ideas across each other.

Say. "Hey, if we had a car accident and I had to run out of my house, what could I do? Do I know how to safely get somebody out of the car, safely hold somebody's neck if it looks like they had an impact injury?" Just list the what-ifs.

What if my son fell and cut his arm? Where am I going to get a bandage from? Where am I going to get a dressing from? Do I know how to apply it? You could even step it up from there and say, "Well maybe we can get together one day this week with a couple of friends and just throw on some triangle bandages, see if we can make a sling, and start your own training. Be creative and think outside the box.

It's nice to say, "Yeah, at $500 I can go take this class. I'm going to buy $200 worth of kit. I'm going to put a kit in my car and I'm going to have a kit on my person at all times." A lot of us don't have that time or money. Try to be creative. A lot of the companies offer samples and stuff like that. Have somebody who is web savvy start hitting the websites and reaching out, "Hey, I'm so-and-so with this group and we like your product but we'd like to maybe see if you could have two or three to test out, if you'd send them to us". A lot of times you can get samples that way and you can put a little bit together.

Doc: There are a lot of training videos on You Tube for all these products. You can actually get quite a bit of knowledge from YouTube as well. You can find training for all your different products from tourniquets to clotting agents and bandages and everything else.

Rob: Cruz, you mentioned thinking about the problems that you're going to encounter. We talked about how it varies by your lifestyle and your environment. It's important that you sit down and you make a list of the problems and the situations that you may encounter. For the most part you're going to have to guess at this, but you might even want to rank them in order of the likelihood of what you're going to encounter. Cuts on your kids, maybe a broken arm, little things, your kid falls out of the tree. There are a lot of relatively simple things that are going to happen, and you're just going to have to take care of things until you get them to an EMT or to the Emergency Room, but for every person they are going to be different. Make a list of those things that may happen, and then make a list of what you're prepared for training-wise and equipment-wise. Fill those needs that are left over.

Cruz: I've learned from some really good guys about being analytical about this stuff. One of the things I always required of my people when we did things state-side was the information for at least three hospitals: their location, their contact numbers, directions from where I'm at, travel times. If I know I'm going to a certain range, I want to know from that range facility: where are the closest three hospitals, where are the closest three ambulances, where are the closest three fire departments, law enforcement, etc.

Doc: Who has Life Flight, is another big one as well.

Cruz: Start those lists! You said you're on a two-wheel most of the time. Well, if you have an accident there's going to be a lot of abrasions. Set up your kit accordingly. Ask yourself, "What can I learn about abrasions? If I'm hitting the ground at 20 miles an hour, how do I need to set up my stuff up?" If I'm in a vehicle, obviously I can carry more stuff. That outside the box thinking.

It's not a matter of is going to happen, it's when is this going to happen. If it's happening do I drive by and say, "Those people look like they need some help. I don't know what to do," or are you that person that's going to stop and say, "Hey, I might not know everything but I'm going to at least try, and this is what I bring to the table,"? Know when you need help, when you need to call 9-1-1. Know when you need more skills than you bring to the table. I think making a list and understanding what your limitations are and what your strong points are will really benefit the end user.

Rob: What you're saying about the contact information especially applies overseas or in unfamiliar territory. A lot of times you're going to have a doctor or a medical facility that you trust more than other doctors or facilities. They may be within a minute or 30 seconds of each other and you want to make sure that you let people around you know which one prefer. Make sure that you have that facility marked as your in-case-of-emergency on your phone also. Who knows? In the US it may be for different reasons. Sure, maybe you trust a different facility more than another, or maybe it's just because your insurance is better at another place, the hospital that's the next block over. Make sure you let people know. Make sure you write it down. Make sure you have it in your phone so that people know your preferences.

Doc: We do a range book when we're going to a certain range. It will include a map and pictures of the front of the hospital or the emergency entrance. Get several pictures on the way so that we know what the landmarks are. Everything looks the same nowadays, and with a Burger King or a Taco Bell on every corner, it's good to have some reference marks to get you there, and also know what you're looking for in unfamiliar territory. The architecture now seems to be to make everything blend in. That's a good idea for overseas as well. When we were working in Jordan, there were definitely some hospitals there that you needed to avoid at all costs. You were probably better with the injury you had than walking in the doors of some facilities. I'm sure you're seeing that in Nepal as well.

Rob: When it comes to emergency situations, a lot of the time it's going to be other people. Think about the odds, there are more people around you than there is of you(just one), so it's important to prepare to help them, but remember that it could just as easily be you. It's important that you also make sure that you prepare and train your loved ones: maybe your wife or even a teenaged child. Make sure that they understand as much as they can and can help you out. Don't do this just for yourself. Don't just study on your own or go to a course alone. Bring the wife along. If you can, bring the family along. If you can, bring your range buddies along. Do what you can to make sure that the people around you learn also, even if it is just for selfish reasons. It's in your best interest.

Doc: And you can also talk things through. I advise people in my classes to take what you learn in this class and go back and have these serious conversations with your wife and your loved ones. "If something happens, this is what I want you to do. If something happens to me, this is what I want you to do." If some sort of combat breaks out, I don't want my wife near me. She knows that she's supposed to get away from me, dial 9-1-1, and describe me to the cops so they know what's going on. She knows that if I get hit and go down, she's not supposed to come to me. She's to get as far away from me as possible. Having those serious conversations are important for medical situations as well. "If this happens, this is what I need you to do" I wholeheartedly agree with you on that. Have those conversations. Have them with your kids as well.

Cruz: When you go through these things together, you're going to bond together as a family. You have that level of trust. It brings you closer together on several different levels, plus you can now have a second set of hands to help you work through the situations and the problems that you have. Rsktkr runs a class where we have spouses come to the class and work together. One of the scenarios we talk about is fighting with your child in your arm. How does that change the techniques that you were going to apply? People's eyes just light up.

When you have your spouse with you and you try to work through this situation, you are worried about their safety and controlling the situation. It lends a different mindset to it and I think the more that you can learn to deal with that, the better your training will be. I have a 17 year old daughter and a 13 year old son, and they both love to be with me, both out at the range and doing other things. It makes for a good time all around and a learning experience. It also gives you that sense of pride and accomplishment after. Okay, I know they can put a bandage on if something happens.

Rob: When game plan, you work out the possible situations, make sure that you bear in mind the reality that you do have a family. It may be an elderly mother or father that you live with. Every person is different and every lifestyle is different, but you should plan it out as much as possible. Prepare for as much as you can, and hope for the best after that. Thanks so much for talking with us about this. I think this is definitely some stuff that'll be helpful.

Medical Emergency Gear

Bryan Black is the Editor-in-Chief at ITSTactical.com. He founded ITS Tactical in 2009 with the help of brothers in the Naval Special Warfare Community.

Rob: Why don't you start off by just giving us a little bit about your background and your qualifications and what you've done.

Bryan: Sure. I spent some time in the Navy. I was there for a few years with Naval Special Warfare. One caveat, though, is that I wasn't a Navy Seal. I just wanted to put that out there. I did make it two-thirds of the way through BUDs. I got through hell week, pool comp, and some of the more difficult evolutions, but I had a gas embolism on a Drager(a closed circuit rebreather) towards the end of second phase that wound up costing me my career in the Navy. I got out shortly after that.

When I got out in 2006, I went back to school for web design and started my own business doing that. I and a couple of buddies of mine had had the idea back in the Navy of doing something like ITS Tactical: a website for skill-set information, e-reviews, and do-it-yourself projects geared toward the military, law enforcement community, and also outdoor enthusiasts. That's where I come from and what I bring to the table with what I write about on ITS Tactical.

Rob: Well, I really love ITS, Imminent Threat Solutions. I really love the title that you've given this, and it does encompass a lot of different things, but it basically focuses on protecting people and taking care of them. There's a lot of different aspects of that, and your site covers so much information. There's quite a variety there, but one of the things that I see that you do cover quite well and talk about quite often is medical preparedness. You have even put together this ETA trauma kit. Tell us a little bit about that.

Bryan: What we try to advocate on ITS is always being prepared in any situation, and a lot of what's overlooked today is the medical aspect of things. I got with a buddy of mine that's still on the teams(he's an 18 Delta corpsman) and we developed a kit that was based on what he was issuing to his guys. We wanted to make something like that available for everybody. We do have a military/law enforcement only version of the kit, but essentially it treats the three leading causes of death in the field. Those have been determined by the Tactical Combat Casualty Care guidelines: extremity hemorrhage (severe bleeding), tension pneumothorax(sucking chest wound), and airway obstruction. You have to establish that airway to keep the patient alive.

Those are the three areas that the kit covers. It's not a boo-boo kit. It doesn't have band-aids or Neosporin. It's really a trauma kit. It's made to treat those three leading causes of death, and those three leading causes of death are so overlooked today it's not even funny. Most police departments out there are solely dependent on EMS to arrive on the scene to treat them. I still can't believe departments don't at least equip their guys with a tourniquet and a pack of combat gauze, which I see as the minimum to really survive.

Our kit has components that treat those three leading causes of death. You've got combat gauze, which is a hemostatic agent. It can be stuffed into a wound cavity, and coagulates and stops the bleeding. You've got halo chest seals, which are to treat a tension pneumothorax, gunshot wounds. Most of the time when you get shot you've got an entrance wound and an exit wound. The halo chest seal is to seal that cavity, both in the front and the back. There are two seals in that package. We've got a decompression needle. We advise that you get some training. Some of these items in the kit aren't necessarily things that you may know how to use right out of the box. Obviously you don't want to go stabbing someone's chest with a needle if you don't know what you're doing. We definitely advocate training behind a lot of what we do and what we sell.

You've got an airway, which is a nasopharyngeal airway. It's an adjunct, so if you do have a loss of a portion of your airway, that nasopharyngeal airway is to adjunct that and to re-establish that airway. You've got an Israeli bandage, which is essentially a pressure dressing. It's got a standard Ace wrap that can be used for anything from a sprain to a compression wrap if necessary. It has Z-packed gauze, which is essentially just a package of gauze that you stuff into a wound cavity to stop bleeding and a combat casualty card if you have to mark a patient to move them to higher echelon care. That will help the higher echelon care know what you've already done to the patient. It's got a pair of gloves, just to protect yourself, a pencil, and a contents list, too. So that's essentially the kit in a nutshell.

Rob: You talked about how this covers the three leading causes of death. Are those the three leading causes of death in a combat situation or just in general?

Bryan: They come from the combat situation but they are really applicable if you're carrying a firearm. Even departments in law enforcement are starting to adopt this T-

CCC stuff(Tactical Combat Casualty Care guidelines). They're starting to institute this into their departments because these three leading causes of death, carry over from combat and are applicable to any situation you're in with gunshot wounds.

Rob: So gunshot wounds, puncture wounds, even a serious car accident, having something like this on hand would be helpful for sure?

Bryan: Even in a car accident you can have something puncture your chest and essentially create a sucking chest wound, just like a bullet could. So yeah, it could be used for that.

Rob: Obviously this is something that any civilian should have with them while they're at the range or out shooting. Do you see people that are picking these up and carrying these with them most of the time, or do they stash them in a vehicle at work, at home, etc. How do most people handle keeping this with them all the time?

Bryan: We advocate keeping it on your person, whether that's in a range bag if you're on a range, whether that's in a go bag if you're in your vehicle, or whether it's even in a cargo pocket when you're at the range or any time you're shooting. There's a wide array of reasons or methods that people use to carry these. I've seen everything. We even make a pouch that can go on standard molly gear. You can store the kit either sealed in the vacuum sealed packaging it comes in, or you can break it apart and carry each item individually in our kit. We've tried to cover the gamut of how people carry it.

Rob: Let's talk about training that can go with this. Having the gear on hand makes it available for someone else that may know how to use it also. There are a lot of different situations where it would be helpful, but what kind of training is the minimum that somebody would want to get to be able to use all this stuff to its fullest potential?

Bryan: I would say that at a minimum, a good first aid CPR class is highly encouraged before you wind up treating anybody for anything. There are the Good Samaritan Laws in most states. I honestly think they're in every state now. That kind of covers you from liability of providing care to somebody in an emergency situation. So if you happen to come upon a car wreck or something like that, and you actually do take the time to render aid to somebody, you're protected in that sense, but we obviously advocate getting good training to know how to use some of these things in the kit.

That's not to say you can't just have this on you. We advocate that even having these tools on you could save your life. The person that could come along to treat you might know how to use these things. Having them on you might save your life or someone else's around you. I'd say at a minimum, get first-responder type training. The American Red Cross is a great place to go for CPR and first-aid training. Then, a step above that, you can get into classes by medical professionals. We've partnered with Lone Star Medics. It's a company in Texas that provides medical training. They do some stuff out of the norm that we really advocate like fighting with the rifle while rendering aid and learning medical techniques.

I think medical training is very important. It's an area that's often neglected in training. A lot of people know how to shoot a gun and seek out training for learning to shoot a gun, but they don't understand that there's more to it than that. Behind almost every bullet that's fired is a wound somewhere.

Rob: This is equipment that's going to save your life. It's for critical wounds, things that are a big deal. Like you said, this is not a boo-boo kit. This is the big time insurance. This is what'll cover you when you're hurt seriously.

The majority of what happens is not going to require this kit, so I'm sure that you also want to carry extra stuff over and above this. I don't know if you want to call it medical necessarily, but what other medical-related equipment or gear would you recommend for the smaller stuff, the boo-boos?

Bryan: Everybody has a box of Band-aids, and Band-aids are great. They cover up a wound, but really, most non-life-threatening wounds can be treated with a basic pressure dressing. Direct pressure is essentially what stops all bleeding.

Rob: Duct tape

Bryan: Yeah, honestly you can use duct tape. Use some gauze, hold pressure on that, and then use duct tape for a pressure dressing. If you were going to either supplement our kit or downgrade from the kit, try to actually carry a tourniquet and a pack of combat gauze with you wherever you go. That's my bare minimum. There's a lot you can do with that. The combat gauze, even though it's impregnated with the kaolin, the hemostatic agent, can actually be used as regular gauze as well. You can still pack a wound cavity with it, even if it may not be life threatening bleeding. You can also use it for a surface wound by just laying it over the wound and wrapping a pressure dressing around it, or duct tape as you said.

Rob: It doesn't have to be a huge gouged out wound.

Bryan: Correct. Just carrying some basics on you is all that's necessary in most situations. The hemostatic agents are really where it's at today. Having the ability to stop bleeding with an anticoagulant like combat gauze is just a great thing. It comes down to a pack of combat gauze(roughly $40), and you throw a tourniquet on top of that(maybe another $25-$30). In the long run, what's your life worth? That's what you have to ask yourself A lot of people get put off by the pricing on some types of medical equipment. The underlying question shouldn't be, "How much does it cost?" The question is: What is your life worth? That's what you need to ask yourself. That has nothing to do with whether you buy our kit it's about having the necessary supplies on you to treat yourself or those around you.

Rob: Don't forget those around you, especially your family, your children, your wife, etc. It's important that you prepare to take care of them also. The technology that's out there really is amazing to me. I've just seen some videos of what these hemostatic agents and the newer gauze can do as far as stopping bleeding. If any of you have seen any sort of a serious wound, it'll blow your mind how much blood can come out. I agree that having gauze on hand with you all the time would be the absolute minimum. Something with a hemostatic agent would be that much better. It really does make a huge difference when you've got a major wound.

Bryan: Sure, absolutely.

Rob: I appreciate you going through the kit here. That's the main thing I wanted to cover along with the three leading causes of death. With your kit, what size are we talking about? How much weight, how much space does this take up?

Bryan: All the versions of the kit are vacuum sealed down small enough to be able to put into a cargo pocket. So that gives you a rough idea of the size. If you're carrying a pack of combat gauze and a tourniquet on its own, they can easily be put into the back pocket of a pair of jeans. If you're talking about the essentials, there's not much space required at all.

Rob: I hope people will check it out: itstactical.com. You can find it right in the shop. Also, lots of other interesting goodies there too. Bryan, I appreciate you taking the time to talk to us about this. Thanks!

Bryan: Thanks for having me, Rob. I appreciate it.

Timepiece Features and Recommendations

Thomas Carey is a timepiece enthusiast who is passionate about helping people find the watch that is perfect for them. He is based in Pontiac, Illinois and sells high-quality watches from his online storefront: thecgacompany.com

Rob: First of all, why don't you tell us a little bit about your background and why you're qualified to talk about watches.

Thomas: I sell watches, but I've really been interested in watches ever since I was real young. I got my first watch from a grandmother of mine that bought it as a birthday gift for me when I was maybe 11 or 12 years old, and in addition to selling the watches, which I've been doing for about four or five years, I've also worked with a couple of brands behind the scenes, helping them with designs, or locating manufacturers to make their product, or sourcing movements and things like that.

Rob: Ultimately, a watch is a tool to tell you what the time is and to keep you on schedule but there's so much more to it. When you're a little kid, you go and pick up your first watch off of a rack at a big box department store. Maybe you've got cartoon characters on it, but as you grow up you have different needs and you may want to look for something that's going to last you longer than several months or a year. You may want something that's going to be an heirloom. There are different reasons that people want to move up to a higher quality watch. What's the main reason that you see most people wanting to move up to something more than a cheap watch they get in a big box store?

Thomas: It's like having a finer quality firearm or a higher quality tool. After a while you get tired of having something that just barely does the job and doesn't do it very well. In the case of the watch, when you have a problem with it later on, like a silly strap needs to be replaced, they'll tell you just buy another one.

All those things get old to people after a while. People are kind of tired of the kind of the throw-away society that we live in, and they want to have things that are going to last, something that they may be able to pass down to a son or a daughter.

Rob: In my case, sometimes you'll buy a watch, maybe it's even a cheap watch at Wal-Mart and you become attached to the watch. I guess you'd say it's sentimentality, but you end up having to throw this watch away. With a quality watch, once you get attached to it and you get used to it and you start to enjoy it, you could actually hang onto it for a while.

Thomas: You see that a lot, especially when people are just looking for a simple replacement watch strap. A lot of times, the strap costs as much money as the watch. So you have to decide, "Do I just buy another watch or do I replace the strap", and with a lot of the lower priced watches, they're battery powered. So then you're thinking, "If I haven't replaced the battery yet, how much longer do I have with that, and then how much is that going to cost?" People go through that with a lot of things, and ultimately end up throwing it away, and they really don't want to do that because later they end up purchasing something new. You're forever stuck that same cycle.

Rob: The bicycle will get you across town. It'll meet your needs, but the Ferrari is so much more comfortable and so much nicer. When it comes to watches, you can spend as little or as much as you want. There are many different levels of quality, comfort, and practicality that you're can choose from.

Thomas: There are so many factors that come into play. First of all, consider your budget. There's no sense in starting to look until you have a budget set. Invariably, you will fall in love with something that costs more money than you are able to spend. That can be frustrating.

You also need to know what you want the watch to do. Most people just want the watch to tell time, but there are so many things that come into play. From a tactical aspect, it's probably a good idea to get a watch with tritium tubes. A lot of people that are in the military, law enforcement, emergency services, or serving as firefighters end up in a situation where they are in dark places and need to tell time. With a conventional watch, if it hasn't got enough charge, it won't glow, but a watch with tritium tubes will always glow.

Rob: What's the half-life of tritium?

Thomas: The half-life is like 10 or 12 years.

Rob: It'll last a long time.

Thomas: It really does. That's one factor. There are so many other factors after price. What is my job? How much wear and tear is there on my equipment?" If you're in a high stress job as far as wear and tear on your equipment, then you're going to have to look at a watch that's a lot more durable.

Rob: Now, let's start with that. When it comes to durability, you want something that's going to keep on ticking. You want something that's just going to work. Most watch brands, once you get over a certain price point, you're not really going to have to worry about it breaking on its own, but there are other aspects. If you're a diver, you want it to be able to handle going under water to certain depths. If you work in a shop, the thing might get hit or might get dropped on hard floors. You are looking for extra impact resistance. How do you go about researching this? Are they all pretty much the same across the different brands?

Thomas: They're really not. A lot of things are standard at certain price points. There are certain price points where you would expect that it would be a stainless steel case with a sapphire crystal. That's usually when it's north of $350 or north of $400. You will find at that price point, that there are many watches which can be had with PVD coating which may be a good idea for someone in tactical situation.

Rob: Help me out. What is PVD coated?

Thomas: PVD coating is a protective coating that can be put on stainless steel. The real popular color is a matte black. A lot of the time, it actually looks like a polycarbonate, but it's really a stainless steel that's PVD coated. It is much more resistant to scratches then bare stainless which can be scratched fairly easy. Titanium is actually worse. Titanium scratches if you look at it. That's probably not a great option for people looking for durability. The PVD cuts down on the scratches and it gives you a non-reflective finish. It really dulls it out and doesn't reflect like the bare steel will.

Rob: Thank you for going back and clarifying that for me. Let's get back to what you were talking about. You can expect different specifications, different characteristics at different price points.

Thomas: If you're only looking at a watch that's about $60 to $350, it's probably going to have a mineral crystal or an acrylic plastic crystal on it. The crystal is the glass that you look through. The acrylic is going to scratch like crazy, and you see that on a lot of the cheap watches. Pretty soon, it's got so many scratches on it you can't even see what time it is. You really want to stay away from a watch that has a plastic crystal. You really want to go with one that, at the very least, has a mineral crystal. Mineral crystals will still scratch, just not nearly as badly as the plastic crystal will.

Rob: So where do we normally see a price break between the plastic and the mineral crystal?

Thomas: You see the plastic on the cheap $20-$40 watches, sometimes even up to $60. Above $60, you're pretty much running into mineral crystals at that point, but you need to look at the specs to really see what you're getting.

Rob: And once you move up around $350, that's where you're getting into the sapphire crystal?

Thomas: Possibly, but sometimes you're still looking at a mineral crystal. In Europe the mineral crystal is actually far more popular. That's because they're not as fragile as a sapphire crystal. The sapphire crystal is harder and more scratch resistant, but also more brittle. They look at the mineral crystal to be a better compromise, while here in the US we would rather have a sapphire crystal because you're just not that likely to get a scratch on a sapphire crystal.

Rob: How different is the mineral crystal from the sapphire crystal? It's obviously a huge step up in performance and scratch resistance from the plastic to the mineral crystal, but what about from the mineral crystal to the sapphire?

Thomas: Well, visually you won't see a difference at all, but as far as scratches go, you will scratch a mineral crystal. You're just going to. With the sapphire, you're probably not going to. That's going to be the most noticeable thing for most people. For people that are really rough on their equipment and their watches get bounced around and knocked into things, you might want to go with the mineral crystal because it's more resistant to impacts and would be less likely to chip. If a company boasts about shatter-proof crystals, that tells you that it's most likely a mineral crystal. If they say it's scratch-proof and shatter-proof, the crystal is mineral with a coating that is supposed to make is as resistant to scratches as sapphire. However, with a lot of watches the crystals are somewhat protected, especially on the dive watches where the bezels protect them a little bit. When you take a hit, a lot of times you get lucky and it'll hit on the bezel and not the glass. I really don't see a lot of sapphire crystals that have been damaged to be honest. For that matter, I really don't see a lot of mineral crystals that are chipped, either. I do see maybe 2 out of 5 tactical watches that have mineral crystals which do have scratches on them. In some cases there are so many scratches you can scarcely tell what time it is. The crystals can be replaced if they are damaged and on a higher quality watch it's generally worth doing that.

Rob: So it's not as big a deal as people think, but it's better to know what you are getting into.

Thomas: I think that the difference is not as great as a lot of people would like to make you believe. The difference in the scratch resistance is huge. The sapphire can be scratched, but it's really unlikely. People that are into watches here in the US pretty much demand sapphire crystals on the more expensive watches.

Rob: We touched on the finish just a little bit and you mentioned the matte black finish that is going to limit reflectivity and make it more abrasion resistant. What other types of finishes are there? What options do people have?

Thomas: Some of the higher end Swiss watches and some of the higher end boutique brands(really small brands that a guy with a dream starts up on his own) are switching to DLC, which has been used more in knives and firearms. The finishes that are being used in watches are following say the knife industry, but they're way behind. The knife industry, they had PVD coatings on their blades to make them black several years ago. Now they have switched. Companies like Kershaw and Spyderco on their higher end models are going into the better DLC coatings. Now the higher end watch companies are starting to switch to that too. Honestly the brand I deal with most that has a lot of experience with both those coatings, Lum-Tec, has found that their vendor actually does a better job with the PVD coating than the DLC, even though the DLC is supposed to hold up better and be more wear resistant. The DLC tends to be shinier too. It's a more reflective than the PVD is.

Rob: So the PVD, like any coating, is only as good as how well it's applied. That's an important aspect to look at.

Thomas: Yeah, that definitely is.

Rob: Now, any coating, dealing with firearms and knives, any coating will scratch. If you use the right metal and you have the right amount of force with something sharp, it will scratch, but it's just about finding something that coats it well enough that it limits the scratches, or makes it difficult to scratch. Hopefully you aren't out there rubbing your watch on the asphalt, but occasionally you're going to bump into or knock something, and you want a coating that's going to make sure that you limit the scratches as much as you can.

Thomas: The PVD will really limit the scratches, but one of the downsides is, especially with the matte black finishes, when you get a scratch in it, that underlying stainless steel really shines through. It's far more annoying to get a scratch in a watch with a PVD finish then to have several scratches in one with stainless steel. With the stainless steel watch, you can take it to a watchmaker and they can polish that out, but with the PVD finish or the DLC, once that's scratched, there's not really a good way to repair it. You basically have to replace the part, or the part would have to be disassembled, totally stripped(very hard to do), and totally re coated.

A lot of people struggle with whether they want to have that PVD coating or the stainless steel. Personally, I have yet to scratch one of my watches with the PVD coating, but I've had customers that have, so I know it happens. It's usually when you hit a sharp corner of steel or a concrete block. You get a little bit of a scratch on it.

Rob: Let's move onto something that most people consider to be the most important part of a watch, and rightfully so. It's the actual timekeeping, the mechanism, the accuracy of the watch itself.

Thomas: There are a variety of movements that you're going to encounter. What I primarily sell are analogue movements and that's where my expertise is. Basically, you have two types. There are the battery powered movements like the quartz movements or the hybrids that are powered by the sun and then you have the purely mechanical movements. That's the major difference that most people will see when they shop for a watch. At the higher price point, upwards of $550, you'll run into the option of getting a mechanical watch. The nice thing about a mechanical watch is that there is no battery to replace.

Rob: Quartz movements are very accurate, right?

Thomas: They are very accurate, but they're not all alike. There are some that are far more accurate than others. A cheap quartz movement is not nearly as accurate as a more expensive quartz movement. So if you see a watch that's priced pretty cheap and has even a "Swiss" quartz movement, and a higher end one, like a Breitling, that has a quartz movement, the accuracy difference will be noticeable. A movement in a cheap watch may lose a few seconds in a week. In a high end watch, the quartz movement may only lose a few seconds in a year on the highest end.

Rob: So let's compare that to a mechanical, an automatic watch.

Thomas: The mechanical movements are just not going to be as accurate as the quartz watches, no matter what anybody wants to tell you. They're not going to be. Most of the reason that people go for the mechanical movements is because of the mechanical aspect of it. They're into mechanical things and it has an allure to it. It's like working with automobiles because you love working with mechanical items. Accuracy-wise, even if you've got a chronometer grade watch it may be plus or minus six seconds in a 24-hour period.

The cheapest quartz watch is still going to be far more accurate than that. Now you even have the watches that are automatically adjusted by the atomic clocks via radio signals. You just won't beat those for accuracy. The mechanical movement is not something that you go to because of the accuracy. It's usually a movement that the more passionate watch enthusiasts go into. For the average person, I really don't recommend it. Most of your readers are probably going to be better served with a solid quartz movement. It'll hold up to abuse better over the long haul, and it's cheaper to service as well.

Rob: How is somebody going to tell, other than price, whether they're getting a high quality quartz movement? You're not going to hang around the store and be able to check it over the course of a week. How are they going to be able to tell?

Thomas: You're better off sticking with reputable brands that you know well. The reputable brands that have been around and stood the test of time are using the better quality products in their watches. They have a reputation to uphold. Stay away from brands that are mostly into fashion and also have watches on the side. They have an inferior movement a lot of times. They're normally a cheap, Chinese movement. Also you can look at the specs if the watch has a Swiss Movement or Japanese Miyota movement they will list it in the spec as it really is a selling point. If they don't list it there is a darn good chance it's Chinese.

Rob: Someone wants to get something that's going to be durable. They want the sapphire face, they want the tritium, they want a high-quality case for the watch, but they want the quartz accuracy. Are there any particular companies or manufacturers that make these? Is this a well-served niche?

Thomas: You can get a pretty good combination of those features from someone like Lum-Tec, except they don't have the tritium tubes. When you put in the tritium tube requirement, you make it difficult. Tritium tubes are tightly controlled. There is actually only one manufacturer in Switzerland that even has the licensing to work with them on the dials and hands. Any watch that you see that says it's Swiss-made and it has tritium tubes is actually being made by only one manufacturer, or at least the dial and hands are, and usually the complete watch. The ArmourLite brand of watches have Tritium tubes, many are PVD coated, and the price for the quality is a solid value.

Rob: Is it hard to find a quartz movement with tritium hands?

Thomas: It's not. Most Luminox watches are that way. They have some autos now, but most of their's are quartz powered. They use high-quality Swiss quartz movements. Their trade-off is that they use mostly mineral crystals on their watches.

Rob: As you're getting into some of these higher end watches, the aficionados care about the mechanical movements because it's a work of art. It's impressive to think that there are a bunch of gears that are actually making this thing run at this level of accuracy. That's where you start to get into the higher prices, right?

Thomas: Yeah, it really is. Honestly, I would advise people not to even consider buying a watch with a mechanical movement that was under $400. The quality of the movement isn't going to be all that great and below $400 you would probably be better off with a quartz movement.

Rob: When it comes to a $400 watch, where does most of the money go when it comes to manufacturing and that sort of thing? Which aspects are the most expensive?

Thomas: A major component is the movement, especially with the mechanical watches. It just depends on the type of movement. Quartz movements can be quite expensive or they can be just a dollar or two. A lot of their cost is also in the case.

If it has a stainless steel bracelet on it, it would be in the bracelet as well. The case is actually one of the most expensive components in the watches at that price point, especially when you figure in the things that are on the case like the crystal and bezel, and the labor of assembling everything and pressure testing it all.

Rob: I also wanted to talk about fit. Different watches have different sized faces. There are limitations on even strap sizes. A lot of people are searching, comparing, and eventually buying online. What do they need to know about making sure that a watch is going to fit their wrist?

Thomas: Their best bet is to try to go out locally and try watches, even if they go out to Wal-Mart and try on watches of different sizes. When they find one that fits, they need to find out what the width of the watch is. It's a common measurement. It's basically right across the face from the 6 to the 10 and you don't measure the crown. If you can find out the size of a watch that you've tried on and is really comfortable for you, you want to stay with a size that's close to that. A lot of the stuff that's out there now is big and the heavy. They are real popular with the watch aficionados, but the general public can get really turned off.

I've seen a lot of people that will order something on the internet and it ends up being a lot bigger and heavier then they ever expected a watch to be. They would be best served by going out and actually trying some watches out locally to get an idea of what size is going to feel the best for them.

Rob: What about the bands? What about people that have oversized or undersized wrists? What is the range of most straps, and how are people going to make sure that they fit that way?

Thomas: If you have a wrist that's over eight inches around, and it's not a bad idea to measure that, you could very well have a problem with a watch fitting you. A lot of the straps that come standard with them will just be barely long enough, and you might be on the last hole on the strap. Technically it fits, but the average person's not going to like it. If you have a wrist that's thicker than eight inches, you really have to be looking for a watch that you can probably get an extra-long strap on it. A lot of times that's an extra cost item that you have to come up with on your own.

In most cases, a person with a bigger wrist will be better off going with a metal bracelet or a NATO strap(a one size fits all strap). Either way, both of those options are going to fit. If you have a larger sized wrist, you could very well have a problem with a leather strap or a rubber strap.

With your readers, I would not recommend a leather strap unless they were using it in a dress-type situation. I would really recommend rubber or a metal bracelet. Metal bracelets are more popular in North America than any other strap. This is different from in Europe. The most popular thing in Europe is leather straps. A bracelet costs more initially. Sometimes it's a sizeable difference in the cost, but instead of replacing a strap every year or two, with the bracelet you basically don't have to worry about ever replacing it. So it's really smart to consider getting a watch with a bracelet initially, because in the long run it's going to be less hassle, and price-wise it's going to end up being about the same over time.

Rob: Let's talk about comfort when it comes to straps also. Is a cloth strap or a NATO strap going to generally be any more comfortable then a rubber strap or a bracelet?

Thomas: The NATO straps, in my opinion, are as comfortable as or more comfortable than rubber. It's particularly advantageous in a hot climate. A rubber strap does not breathe, and generally people are wearing the watches pretty tight. You see people end up with heat rash with watches with rubber straps whereas with the NATO strap, it's a nylon strap and it actually breathes. I personally wear a watch with a NATO strap and so does my father. We have access to whatever we want, but usually it'll be a NATO strap because it holds up to the elements really well much like a bracelet does. It's not as good as a bracelet, but it's more comfortable and lighter than a bracelet. When it comes time to replace the NATO strap, you don't need any special tools. The average person can change the NATO strap themselves.

Rob: Is there anything else that we need to cover for someone that's selecting a watch?

Thomas: Especially if you're going to buy online, but this really goes for anything. Don't buy a watch from somebody who isn't an authorized dealer for the brand. If you don't heed my advice and you have a problem, the manufacturer's not going to honor the warranty on it at all. I've encountered that several times over the years. If you're not an authorized dealer, the warranty is void. You're really better off going with an authorized dealer.

Rob: It's not about getting the cheapest watch. You want to make sure that you get what you're paying for. Are there any particular watch brands or models that right now are a particular value? Maybe it's because of public perception or people are unaware of them?

Thomas: Well, a lot of the best values going right now are in the little boutique brands. Lum-tec is one. Prometheus is one. There are several others out there. They don't have the mark-up that the major manufacturers have on their watches. You're not paying for all the layers of sales people, representatives, advertising, etc. The boutique brands seem to be popping up everywhere. Make sure they have a good reputation, and a lot of them do. On the new brands that nobody's ever heard of, you have to know the specs and what is in the watch before you take a chance on something like that.

Rob: So do you have any recommendations? Any of those boutique brands that you have had a good experience with or you know people that have?

Thomas: Lum-tec is one that I carry. Prometheus I have in the past. They're both excellent values. Red Sea is a good one. There are some higher end ones too. Marvin is still a small brand, but they have mostly dress-type stuff. ArmourLite is a good small brand that has the tritium tactical-type watches at a good price. Luminox is a larger brand, but they are still very competitive on their entry point models with polycarbonate cases. That's really a good way to go for a lot of your readers.

Nine times out of 10, I would probably recommend that they buy a ArmourLite, or Luminox because of what you get for the cost. In most cases I would recommend they go with a quartz and not the automatic, and probably a watch with tritium tubes.

Rob: I think we've gotten some practical advice for selecting a watch and these are some tips that will be able to help people. Tell us your web address where people can find your stuff and purchase through you.

Thomas: My web address is www.thecgacompany.com. You can also find us on Facebook. We have a strong presence there: www.facebook.com/cgaco We're also active on some of the forums like Usual Suspects Network, and Luxury 4 Play. That brings up something I want to point out. The smartest thing to do is arm yourself with knowledge. You can gain a lot of knowledge by taking the time and researching on the watch discussion forums. They can tell you, especially with these little boutique brands, which ones to go with and which ones to stay away from. The smartest thing to do is really educate yourself and go to people that know a lot more about watches then you do and ask them questions before you make a purchase.

Rob: Sounds like some good advice. Thank you so much for sharing your knowledge.

Thomas: You're most welcome.

A Performance Writing Tool

Steve Nichols is the Vice-President of sales at Fisher Space Pen Company, an innovative company that manufactures high-performance writing tools for extreme environments.

Rob: I'd like to talk with you today about a subject that's not addressed very much. The importance of a pen or writing utensil is often overlooked in people's everyday carry gear. Pens are used far more often than keys, knives, or lights, yet some people just grab whatever they have available with no thought of something that could serve them better. I know a lot of people that are big fans of your products. I'm sure you deal with a lot of customers one-on-one. Why do people want Space Pens?

Steve: A Space Pen is just about the only pen that writes upside down, under water, in minus 40 degrees below zero up to 250 above, and three times longer then the average pen. It's truly a performance pen. I've had people come up to me and say, "I've gotten in my truck up in Canada where it's 15 below zero first thing in the morning, and I had to write down a phone number or an e-mail address, and I grabbed your pen out of the glove box, and I didn't have to draw circles or warm it up with my hands. It just wrote instantly." I'll have other people say, "When are you ever going to use a pen at 250 degrees above?" I live in Las Vegas. I leave my pens in my car during the middle of day in the sun and the heat. It hits 190 degrees in that car. They don't explode, they don't leak.

They perform instantly, right then and there. When you have people out in extreme weather and they have waterproof or laminated papers and it's raining or misty or snowy and they've got to write down coordinates and document things, our pens perform perfectly for them. If that paper is soaking wet, or if it's raining or snowing on it, the pen writes through that water.

Our pens will write on glass, PVC, or x-ray film. They write on a lot of materials that other pens don't write on. It comes into that performance aspect. When you grab a pen and you've got certain materials to write on, or certain conditions to write under, or even if you're just holding your clipboard up against the wall and you've got to jot down notes, the space pen will write.

Rob: You mentioned, "When are you going to need that?" The answer is: "When you least expect it." That's how it always happens.

Steve: Exactly.

Rob: Going back to writing on unusual materials, that sounds very interesting, because that can actually allow you to not worry about having a marker handy and markers can be even more finicky then normal pens. How does this work? Is this because it's a different ink formulation, or is it because of the design of the ink cartridge? What allows it to do this?

Steve: It's a combination of both. Our ink is called a siskal tropic type of ink. It's a very thick ink. It's almost the consistency of a tar. It's almost like a solid gel. In the pressure sealed refill, the ink, is at the bottom. Then we have a nylon ball, and above the nylon ball, we have nitrogen pressurized to 45 pounds. The Nitrogen is pushing on that ball and pushing on the ink toward the tip. The tungsten steel rollerball at the tip, holds back the ink.

The rolling action of the ball shears a little bit of the ink off and lays it down on paper, films, glass, plastic, or laminates and it lays that ink down right on top of that surface. It dries almost instantly. If you wait about two or three seconds, you can take your finger, run it across that ink, and it won't smudge or smear. That way, if you've got a laminated business card, or even a laminated greeting card that you want to write, it'll just lay the ink down very nicely.

The refill is sealed. When you open up a most pens, you'll see that the top part is empty and as the ink goes down, the air just refills the cartridge. On our refill, the top part of the cartridge is sealed, in between, we have a nylon ball, and then we put pressurized nitrogen in there. As you write with it and the ink goes down, the nitrogen is constantly pressing on that ball, forcing the ink to stay at the tip of the pen. That way, even if the pen is upside down for many hours, it will write instantly. We have our Trekker pen that's designed to hang from a backpack, a vest, a lanyard, and that pen is hanging upside down all the time. The moment you unclip it and start writing, it writes instantly.

Rob: Tell me about the size of this cartridge? From what I hear, it's able to fit in a lot of different types of pens.

Steve: It's easier for us to build one refill size and then build the different pens around it. It's also easier for our consumer and our dealers. That way, if somebody runs out of ink on one of our pens, they just say that they have a Fisher pen. It doesn't matter if it's our 400 Bullet pen or a Capamatrix or AG-7 or whatever. That same refill will fit in all of them. They don't have to cross-reference what type of pen they have from us to find a refill. We do have a fine point, a medium point, and a bold point, and many different colors: blue, black, green, purple, red.

Rob: What is the size of that fine point?

Steve: It varies with the touch of how somebody writes. You can give a medium point to somebody and if they have a real light touch, it almost looks like a fine point on the paper. You can give that same medium point to somebody who presses down heavily on the paper and it will lay down a bolder, wider line. I've noticed that at trade shows when different people will try out our demo pen. It depends on the individual and how much they're pressing down on the paper.

Rob: Is that variation due in part to the actual pressure that's behind the ink? Does the pressure make it easier for it to vary?

Steve: I guess since the pressure's there and that ball is laying down the ink, you can have a very light touch, just rub the pen across the paper, and it'll still lay down the ink. The tolerances on that tungsten steel ball and the tolerances of the refill are so finely tuned that that ball does move very freely with very little resistance. It takes very little effort to have that ball rolling.

Rob: You mentioned that the refill writes about three times as long as the average pen, right?

Steve: The average pen, if you had a sheet of paper long enough, would write about a mile in linear length. Our refill gets a little over three miles worth of linear length.

Rob: Yeah, that's a lot of writing, but the size of the cartridge itself is not oversized?

Steve: No, no. It's actually probably smaller then most of the average refills. It's a bit shorter.

Rob: That makes it very easy to fit in some of these smaller pens that people really enjoy carrying.

Steve: Yes. In some of our refills, we do have a Parker adapter. It's hard for us to say that our refill with the adapters "will fit in this kind of pen" because there are just so many other different manufacturers out there with different model numbers and configurations, but there are a lot of people that might have a favorite pen that was given to them, but they want the performance that we can give them, so they'll put our refill in there.

Rob: There are a lot of different pens that do advertise that they do work with your refills. They're known across the industry as something that's reliable enough for people to recommend to go with their pens. How many different pen designs do you have yourself to go with these refills?

Steve: Oh, boy. That's a very good question. I would guess, between different styles and different colors, probably well over 50.

Rob: Now, the one that I would think is probably the most famous is the Bullet pen, right?

Steve: Yeah, that's correct. Our number 400 chrome Bullet pen is our number one seller. That was featured in the Museum of Modern Art in New York City for its iconic design, and still today it's our number one seller.

Rob: It looks beautiful and I like it. Can you give us some basic dimensions?

Steve: What's nice about that Bullet pen is that when the cap is on, it folds down very small. It's only about three and three-quarter inches long. That's especially nice for a fellow if he has a T-shirt on or golf shirt that doesn't have a shirt pocket. You can put that pen in your pocket, and since the cap is on it and it's only three and three-quarter inches long, it fits very nicely in your pocket. You can sit down and you're not going to worry about stabbing yourself. When you take the cap off and put it on the other end of the pen to write, the pen is a touch over five inches long, which makes it about a normal sized pen. The size makes it very nice for everyday carry. The cap just pulls straight off and slides on the opposite end for writing.

Rob: The cap is a little bit longer than most caps and it extends to a little more than five inches when you put it on the back?

Steve: Correct.

Rob: Those of you that have dealt with small pens know that small pens are very nice because they're very easy to carry, yet with a lot of small pens, you're not able to grip and control them comfortably. When you get up to five inches with the cap on the back, you're talking about something that'll fit your hand properly.

Steve: Yeah. It'll rest on just about on the knuckle of your forefinger, on the side of your knuckle there.

Rob: You're not going to have to free float that tail like you would on some of these other small pens.

Steve: That's important. I hold my pen incorrectly and I've grabbed some of these other small pens to write. You have to grip them much tighter, and after writing for a few minutes your hand gets very tired. When the pen expands to the normal length, you can just write with it normally all day long and you don't have to grip it very tightly. In fact, you can grip it fairly lightly because the ink flows out so easily.

Rob: Let's talk about carrying methods. I assume you have clip options?

Steve: Sure. I'll be at a trade show, talking to consumers, and they'll say, "What pen would you recommend me using?" I'll say, "Well, this is going to be a stupid question, but I'm going to ask you, 'How do you use your pen?'" They'll say, "To write," and I'll say, "A better way to ask it is, 'How are you going to carry your pen?'" If it's going to be a desk pen or something that's in your briefcase or your binder, we do have some click action pens that have more a refined executive look; something substantial to show that you're a person of prestige.

That pen still contains our standard pressurized refill. If you're a person that's going to throw that pen in your pocket, I recommend our 400 series because it doesn't take up any room. The ladies like all the different decorative colors and they throw those in their purse. It's almost a fashion accessory. They pull it out and it has that iconic design with a very unique color. We have our Trekker which is designed to hang from a backpack, a vest, a lanyard, or a belt loop. That way when you're out in the cold and the snow and you've got gloves on, and you need to grab a pen to document something, you just snap that off and write on whatever you've got handy. A lot of it is how you're going to carry the pen, and even what type of image you want to portray. All those pens take the exact same pressurized refill and all of them write upside down, under water, 30 degrees below zero, and three times longer then the average pen.

Rob: So going back to the Trekker. That's a great options for a lot of people that like to throw stuff on their keychain. It's three and three-quarters inches long. It's about the same size as the Bullet but it's got the integrated hole where you can attach it right to your keys. Going back to the clip, as far as the Bullet Pen or something in that same small form factor, what do you have? Do you just have a separate clip that you would put over that, or do you have anything integrated?

Steve: Most of the people buy that plain without the clip, just because of the way the design is, but we do have clips that we sell with it. They are a press fit. If somebody has a Bullet pen that they want a clip on, they can buy our clip separately and just press fit it on there. They'll have the option of the clip for that pen. All of our other pens, except for the Trekker, have a clip already attached to them.

Rob: So other than the Bullet pen and the Trekker, everything else has a clip integrated. If you were going to buy a Bullet pen and you want to carry it in your pocket clipped, you would have to purchase that separately?

Steve: You can buy that with or without the clip when you order it.

Rob: Are there any other details that we left out here?

Steve: One other thing to remember is that we're US owned, US made, and we do everything right here in Boulder City, Nevada. We also have a lifetime guarantee and warranty with our product, and we stand behind them unconditionally.

Rob: If you want to check out the pens, you can go to spacepen.com. Thanks so much for talking with us here. I appreciate it.

Steve: Thank you very much.

17644011R00099

Made in the USA
Lexington, KY
19 September 2012